Hatha Yoga Class at Bad Kissingen, West Germany.

Photo by Dietmar Hannebohn

MAKING EVERY MOMENT COUNT
An Illustrated Yoga Guide for Everyone

Carolyn Davis

CSA PRESS, *Publishers*
Lakemont, Georgia
30552

Standard Book Number: 0-87707-225-6

Asanas on pages 102, 123, and 136 by Roy Eugene Davis

Photos by Ron Lindahn

Printed for the publisher by CHB Printing & Binding
Lakemont, Georgia 30552

CONTENTS

Preface

MAKING EVERY MOMENT COUNT

In these times of increasing interest in health, improved function, and the possibilities of vital living, the practice of *Hatha Yoga* is becoming ever more popular. Hundreds of thousands of men and women daily pursue a regime of *Hatha Yoga* geared to their personal requirements. The benefits can be many: self-confidence; improved body function and a healthier appearance; increased vitality and a renewed sense of the joy of living; relaxation at deeper than conscious levels; a brighter mental state; and the opportunity for true self-discovery. These benefits can be important to all who desire to live creatively and with a minimum of stress. For everyone, *Hatha Yoga* practice can be the foundation for the journey on the path to greater inner awareness. These practices awaken vital energies and challenge one to the ideal of living a truly conscious life moment to moment. Those who see *Hatha Yoga* practices merely as exercises leading to improved health will, of course, benefit. But those who see beyond the surface benefits can learn to awaken to a new quality of living, that of living totally in the moment and observing the play of life, while participating fully and joyfully. Such conscious participation makes possible a life of freedom, wherein one is no longer victimized by emotions or environmental influences. This latter group of *Hatha Yoga* practitioners are the aware ones who care enough to want to *make every moment count* in their lives.

WHAT IS HATHA YOGA?

Hatha Yoga is the practice of awareness: the process of being totally involved with the body while practicing various postures, breathing exercises, and relaxation techniques. It is the time one spends each day with himself, allowing no outside intrusion from anyone or anything. It is a way of learning to focus all the attention on present-time awareness, not on what will be done the rest of the day, activities planned for the future, or on any internal conflict. It is the experience of joy and complete attention right where one happens to be. No one can realistically expect to function efficiently and live happily in his world, if he does not first allot time for himself to become self-contained and centered within. Then, looking outwardly from the center of his being and perceiving correctly, he can intelligently and purposefully direct his attention toward his responsibilities. One's first responsibility should always be to his own self. His life then becomes a real contribution and service to the world he lives in, for, in such a way, he will see his destiny unfolding each day with purpose and the conscious knowing that all is well.

Hatha Yoga is the foundation for all the other *Yogas*, focusing attention on the body and everything that happens within it during practice. *Yoga* comes from the Sanskrit word *yug*, which means to join or to bind; union with. *Ha* refers to the sun current, which flows in the right side of the body, and *tha* to the moon current, which flows in the left side. Thus, in *Hatha Yoga*, the goal is to balance the flow of both the currents in the central passageway (called *sushumna*), so that everything in the system flows evenly and in harmony. The body is then in complete balance, the breath flows evenly throughout the system, all the currents in the body are in harmony, and there is complete tranquillity between mind, body, and soul.

The various systems found in the *Yoga* teaching are for the purpose of meeting individual needs. The goal of all *Yoga* practice is enlightenment or God-realization. *Hatha Yoga* strengthens and purifies the body, awakens vital-forces, and gives mental control and great powers of concentration. *Bhakti Yoga* is the way of love, the way of surrender to God and attunement with all people and all expressions of life. *Karma Yoga* is the way to liberation of consciousness as a result of selfless constructive activity. Without compulsive urgency and without resistance to doing his duty, a person who is possessed of understanding attends to his duties with selfless conscious attention. *Jnana Yoga* is the way of wisdom and discernment. As a result of careful examination of any problem, the person of discernment learns to see through the problem to the solution. One who sees through the illusion of his own personality knows clearly his reality as a Pure Being.

Yoga is the intentional discipline that emerged from the religious philosophy known as *The Eternal Religion*. The scriptures upon which this philosophy is based are known as the *Vedas*. *Veda* means "revealed truth." *The Eternal Religion* is simply the way to harmonious living in order to experience true fulfillment in line with personal destiny. Other religious philosophies may have preceded *The Eternal Religion*, but records are not available to us. *Yoga*, however, can be practiced by one regardless of his religious affiliation. *Yoga* does not require that a person accept any teaching on faith alone. In this system we are invited to practice the methods in order to see for ourselves if they will be useful in our quest for increased awareness and greater understanding. Since yogic procedures contribute to self-actualization, it is the experience of many that such involvement also contributes to a greater appreciation of one's personal or traditional religious philosophy. The *Light of the Vedas* filtered down through the ages from ancient India. One stream of influence flowed through Greece and into Europe and another stream flowed through Tibet, China, and Asia.

When a person performs any activity in his daily life (no matter how simple it may be) with conscious intent, he is practicing *Yoga*. Most people know of others whose lives appear to run smoothly on all levels regardless of what transpires about them, and it is certain that such self-contained persons are perfect examples of *Yoga*, even if they have never heard the word before. Thus, one who decides to practice *Yoga* is not asked to change his lifestyle or to renounce the comforts in life to which he has been accustomed. Many are familiar with the *yogis* of the Himalayas who do live austere lives as renunciates, while practicing certain prescribed rituals and waiting upon realization that will satisfy their personal quests and reasons for being. But this is a choice of lifestyle for these *yogis* and certainly not a requirement for the average person to practice *Yoga*. The appeal of *Yoga* is that it offers exactly what so many are missing today: sensible guidelines for intelligent, thoughtful living; logical ways to deal with challenging moments in life; and answers to such basic questions as "Who am I really?" and "Why am I here?"

Truth has been and will always be the same. The words used to describe it in different cultures may vary, but Truth (Reality) itself never changes. It may become clouded by men's perceptions, but it is always there for one to see and hear. And Truth is applicable to every area of living. The serenity that real knowledge brings is especially desirable with the hectic pace of life today. Many people have the material comforts they need, but they may lack real purpose and understanding about life and the life-process. And they have forgotten how to become still and remain self-contained. Their energies and activities have become so scattered that they have become frantic, with no idea how to begin to put order and purpose back into their lives. *Yoga* can supply such answers and offer the way.

It is always useful for one who follows any path of *Yoga*, such as *Hatha Yoga*, to realize that it is based on a most authentic system, one that owes its beginning to one of the oldest philosophies of existence and being known to man. This is the reason it has survived for as long as it has and the reason it will continue to grow and be known in the future, as more and more people seek and find the answers to a conscious way of living.

"Nothing can bring you peace but yourself."
— Ralph Waldo Emerson

DIET AND BODY CLEANSING

Since one deals primarily with the body in *Hatha Yoga*, before the actual practice of *asanas* (the Sanskrit word for postures) begins, the importance of diet and body cleansing must be understood. The body should be clean, both internally and externally. If the body is toxic, one may find it uncomfortable, if sometimes not impossible, to practice the postures. It is also difficult to get in tune with one's self and be the witness to all that is occurring if a distressed part of the body demands a major portion of one's attention. Most people see to external cleansing of the body but may fail to realize there is need for internal cleansing as well. For instance, the nasal passages and mucous membranes can become clogged with mucus, due to improper diet, poor health, or changing weather conditions and a corresponding weakness in these parts of the body. A simple way to clean these passages is by flushing water through each side of the nose. A bowl of warm water (with a small bit of salt added so as not to irritate the membranes) can be filled and the water then sniffed gently while cupped in the palm, first through the left nostril and then through the right. The water should be allowed to run down behind the throat and out the mouth. This process will not only cleanse the passages but will also stimulate the optic nerves and make the eyes brighter and clearer. The tongue can be cleaned each morning upon arising by scraping with a spoon. This removes waste matter that has accumulated during sleep and gives the body that much less initially with which to contend each morning. The teeth should be cleaned thoroughly each day (and each time one eats) with a brush and dental floss to prevent the build-up of plaque, which can lead to tooth decay and eventual gum disease. Correct brushing and flossing, as a dentist can demonstrate, is an invaluable aid to good health.

There may also be a need for intestinal cleansing, especially if eating habits have been poor and elimination faulty and if waste matter has accumulated in the system throughout the years. This alone can contribute so much strain to the physical body that the mental attitude can become negative. Such knowledge, when confronted for the first time by many people, is often shocking to them, but it should be looked at honestly and realistically. Cleansing can be accomplished in two ways. One way is with enemas, to help the cleansing process off to a quick start. A longer but more complete way is with a cleansing diet, which will thoroughly clean out the intestinal tract in a few weeks. An example of such a useful diet is as follows: each day is begun with a small portion of fresh or stewed fruit. A fresh green salad is selected for lunch (with a variety of vegetables), with the salad again repeated at supper along with the addition of brown rice (perhaps seasoned with onions and soy sauce). One can make his own salad dressing, such as olive oil and lemon juice seasoned with garlic. Lightly steamed vegetables can be substituted at dinner in place of a salad. (Liquids should not be consumed at mealtime, as they tend to interfere with digestion.) In only a few day's time on such a diet, one will notice a new lightness in his body and an increase in his energy. At the end of such a diet, the body will be thoroughly cleansed, and one will be inclined to select only small amounts of nutritional foods when hungry. The mental outlook will become positive, and there will be a definite feeling of *all-rightness* in the body. After the body has been cleansed, it is useful to keep it that way with a well-balanced, sensible diet. A correct diet also helps to adjust body weight and makes performance of the *asanas* easier. A clean body will always tell one when it is hungry and what it would like to eat; all that is necessary is to *tune in*, listen to the body, and learn to read its signals. Many people are out of touch with their bodies. They cannot really *feel* the reality of any part of their bodies or identify with them, and they become completely oblivious to their body signals and needs. It is not desirable to become obsessed with the body, but it should be dealt with in a totally conscious manner.

Eating should not be complicated or dwelled upon unnecessarily. A useful recommendation for diet is to eat live foods in small amounts and proper combination. Sugar, white flour, and processed foods are all foods which most people could do better without. Processed food has very little aliveness left in it. Sugar and white flour have carbohydrates and calories, but the vitamin and mineral content is close to nil, and it is useful to eliminate them from the diet without becoming fanatical about it. Fresh fruits, vegetables, grains, nuts, cheeses: foods such as these can be the mainstays of a healthy diet. It is not necessary to become a vegetarian to practice *Hatha Yoga*, but, after practicing for a length of time, many people do find that their protein preferences turn naturally towards fowl, fish, seafood, or vegetable sources. Most important is to eat live foods in combinations the body can best utilize (fruits and vegetables should not be eaten at the same time, for instance, or fruits and meats together) and not to eat too much or too quickly. Food should always be chewed thoroughly, since the process of digestion begins in the mouth, and one should remember that eating too much, even if it is very nutritious food, can work a hardship on the body. (There are many excellent guides to food and nutrition on the market today, such as Adelle Davis' *Let's Eat Right To Keep Fit*. It is useful to become familiar with one of these to get all the facts straight in the beginning.)

To practice *Hatha Yoga* correctly is to practice while totally *in tune* with one's own body: not ignoring, rejecting, or being afraid of it, but treating the body kindly and with respect. It is, after all, one's vehicle for expression in this world, deserving of care and attention. *Feeling* the body from the inside out, reading its signals, knowing what is going on, getting totally involved in the present moment: these should be the first steps in the practice of *Hatha Yoga*, the practice of awareness.

"To be awake is to be alive."
— Henry David Thoreau

*"Let God use your mind,
your hands and all of
your talents and
natural abilities."*
    — Paramahansa Yogananda

PLANNING THE DAY WITH PURPOSE

One of the most practical steps one can take, along with the decision to practice *Hatha Yoga*, is to plan his day with purpose. This might mean writing down a daily schedule on paper to see exactly how time is spent each day and then how to better utilize it. Many people waste so much of their day in useless activity that the day is over before they realize it, leaving them with no real feeling of accomplishment or contentment with what has transpired. Day after day of this type of living can contribute to feelings of boredom and worthlessness.

Hatha Yoga requires discipline, and continued practice will naturally bring more order and discipline into one's life. But a conscious decision at the beginning to use all one's time constructively can be a tremendous boost. And it is always easy to make such a decision when first starting out on a new project and motivation is very high.

Getting into the routine of arising early and greeting the day with positive expectation can be a useful way to begin the day. One should tell himself that this is going to be a wonderful day and then listen to his own advice. Time can first be spent in the bathroom attending to the morning routine, making sure to smile at the familiar and likable reflection in the mirror. Meditating then for twenty to thirty minutes to become centered within will set the tone for the entire day to follow. A light breakfast can be eaten, if one is so inclined, and the day begun with enthusiasm. It is useful to stick with the schedule planned without being rigid, especially if one tends to get off the track and slip into old patterns of laziness at first. After some time has elapsed staying with a purposeful schedule, seeing that something worthwhile is being accomplished each day, even if it is as simple as *completing* daily tasks begun, will contribute to steadiness and purpose, and using time wisely will cease to be an effort; it will have become natural.

The order and discipline that a daily routine brings to living can go a long way towards improvement in one's mental attitude, and this routine need not be a complicated one, but one of simple activities attended to each day with conscious intent. Sometimes it is hard to say what comes first, the change in mental attitude or the decision to put more discipline into daily living. As one wise man has so aptly put it, sometimes it is easier to act our way into positive thinking than to think our way into positive action. One can try it himself and see what happens.

Time should be allotted each day for sitting quietly and reflecting while alone. This will enable one to keep his day well-ordered and all activities occurring with ease, harmony, and balance. It is useful, also, to walk outside in the natural sunlight at least thirty minutes every morning and afternoon, without eyeglasses if at all possible. This is very energizing for the system and good for the eyes. It introduces all the colors of the spectrum into the body and is necessary for good health and balance in the body. *Asanas* are best practiced daily: morning, evening, or whenever most convenient. Some type of exercise (in addition to the *Yogasanas*) to increase the heartbeat and circulation is vital to good health also. Tennis, jogging, golf, swimming: one should pick out his favorite and stick with it. Often a little bit of physical exercise is the best thing for the pent-up feelings resulting from simple tension in daily living.

In the evening hours, one can sit quietly and meditate again to alleviate the pressures of the day and to insure that the day's ending will be calm and serene. Dinner should be a quiet time, with those partaking entering into good fellowship and renewing family ties. Evening hours can be times of quiet recreation and family togetherness. Finally, the reading of inspirational material can be a thoughtful way to end the day. Sleep will then follow naturally and easily, with the last thoughts being of God.

"God obligeth no man to more than
he hath given him ability to perform."
— The Koran, Chap. 65

*"God respects me when I work
But he loves me when I sing."*
             – Tagore

OUTLINES FOR PRACTICE

There are a few simple guidelines for practicing *Hatha Yoga*. Practice time is best approached in a positive, relaxed, open frame of mind. This is not a time to think. It is a time *to be*. One should imagine and let himself be in tune with all his surroundings and flowing with life. In this receptive mood, he can find a quiet spot, with no music and as little sound as possible. Total attention and quietness are necessary to get clear and inside one's self. A special blanket or mat used only at these times can contribute each day towards this receptive attitude (especially if it is a wool blanket, which acts as a natural insulation for the body and tends to keep body currents circulating within).

The time of day one practices is an individual decision; in the morning, practice can help raise the energy level and get the day off to a good start; but the body is not so stiff later in the day, and late afternoon practice can encourage the body to relax and the mind to release any tension accumulated during the day's activities.

As long as clothes are loose and comfortable and do not bind anywhere on the body, one can practice in whatever he chooses. Practice outside in the sunshine in warm weather is advisable whenever possible. The gentle heat from the sun will encourage the body to relax more easily than is usually the case. In cool weather, clothing should be sufficient to keep the joints and extremities of the body warm; warmup suits are excellent choices at such times. They will insure the body not becoming chilled while resting between *asanas* and at the end of practice. Drafts and cold rooms should be avoided during practice. There should be open space without furniture, plants, or objects of any kind to contribute to injury should balance be momentarily lost.

Ample time should be allowed for food to digest after meals and before practice, usually two to three hours after a regular meal. In this way, vital-force in the system can be directed entirely to practice, instead of being diverted to digestion. Although one should not eat just prior to practice, a teaspoonful of honey can give a boost to the system without causing an energy drain on the body while it is being digested. This is intended especially for those people who attend evening *Hatha Yoga* classes after work hours, who may not have time to eat before practice and find their energy reserves a little low.

Practice should be approached each day with regularity, but always relaxed and with total attention. The session need never be hurried, as this neutralizes the benefits of practice and takes one out of the present moment. Two poses executed slowly and completely are preferable to four or five done rapidly and without full attention. At least thirty minutes daily practice time is suggested, while a more intense session of an hour or more at least once weekly can be most useful. The time thus spent should be a private one, entirely for the benefit of the one who is practicing. It is wise to avoid showing other people everything one has learned; this applies especially if others have no interest in *Yoga*. *Yoga* is one's own private experience. It is wiser to be the example of what *Yoga* can do for one than to talk about it. Keeping it a private experience will strengthen one and allow his practice to have much more meaning. Talking too much about it can result in one's losing his initial enthusiasm and motivation.

Many people find that participating in a class, particularly when beginning *Hatha Yoga*, can be useful. Meeting once or twice weekly with the class encourages them and reinforces their practice. Having an instructor, if he or she is truly qualified, can certainly be an asset. The basics can then be demonstrated, and one can be reminded to keep his attention exactly where it should be. But, once one understands how to execute the *asanas* correctly as well as the real purpose behind his practice, the rest is an inside job. The practice of *Yoga* is never limited to a class time, helpful as that may be. It can be done wherever one happens to be, and it is not useful or advisable to become dependent upon a teacher for inspiration to practice. This is the point where one begins to lose touch with himself; next he fails to observe the moments in his life consciously, and it is not long before once sincere interest wanes entirely.

What happens during practice will be up to the individual: his sincerity, the time devoted to practice, and the intensity of interest. Steadiness in practice is best, neither so fired up that enthusiasm burns out quickly nor so negligent that some day it is forgotten altogether. Moderation can be the guideline, as it should be in all areas of living. Progress may sometimes be uneven, or it may seem to be that way. This is natural; some days the body will just bend more easily than others. But the awareness one develops by watching himself along the way is the most important part of practice, inspiring him to continue with more zest and enthusiasm and inclining him toward further observation. He will get to know himself better: what goes on inside his mind and what motivates him. This awakening to the joy of conscious living is what makes the practice of *Yogasanas* so valuable and of real benefit to the practitioner.

Children's Hatha Yoga Class at Lakemont, Georgia.

PHILOSOPHY BEHIND THE PRACTICE

A main point to remember when beginning *Hatha Yoga* practice is that there is never any competition: not with other people, certainly not with one's own self, and not with yesterday's practice session or to-morrow's. Instead, it is a time to be aware of all the changes going on in the body, a time to watch attitudes, emotions, and observations as all these changes occur. One watches these changes from inside the body exactly as an impartial observer would, with no judgment. There is no focus on any long-range goal; all that matters is the present, for that is where everything is observed and learned. When attention is placed upon what is hoped will be accomplished in a certain length of time, contact with the present (with Reality) is actually lost. Physical changes will naturally occur in the body as practice is continued: the body will become more supple and limber. But infinitely more valuable are the lessons learned by observing one's self throughout every step of this process. Learning to observe the body is most useful, being detached and witnessing all that occurs from within the body, the vessel through which one expresses in this world. One is certainly more than his body and mind. He is the eternal *observer* of all the inevitable changes occurring in his life. The body, attitudes, and emotions may change, but one's basic nature does not change. That basic nature is his soul nature, the eternal observer at the composed center within each being that, regard-less of what occurs without, remains ever the same.

Gentleness and non-violence are two key words to guide one in practice. The practitioner of *Yoga* (*yogi*, if a male, and *yogini*, if a female) always treats his body with gentleness and respect. There should never be any pain in the practice of *asanas*, and any such pain should be regarded as a stop signal. All move-ments should be done with the mental image of flowing, as water flows, without strain or sudden jerking of any part of the body. The *yogi* is not violent with his body. He realizes that certain *asanas* sometimes take longer than others to master, and he is content to be *where he is* and to observe what is happening at that particular point. He knows he is exactly where he should be and that his body is responding as it should. There is no hurrying on his part, and there is always moderation in everything he does. Such an outlook requires full attention, and, in *Hatha Yoga*, this full attention is given to every single movement and moment. In return, this attention and concentration gives the practitioner the fullness that each moment of life has to offer, and, until one learns to appreciate the moment, he will never be living fully and consciously.

Disciplining one's self to practice with regularity is necessary for every new student, until it becomes something done automatically. Sometimes the resistance of the mind to practice (or to attend classes) can be stronger even than the body's resistance to bending. And it is crucial at such times to remind one's self that it is he who controls his mind. It is strange that the mind so often resists doing what one knows is useful, almost as if it enjoyed the games being played and the resulting drain in vital-force. But, once the decision is made to stick with practice and any initial inertia is overcome, the knowledge of being in control of one's life and more positive in outlook will reinforce practice, making it a natural part of each day.

One should be certain always to give total attention to practice, to tune in with the body and notice how he actually *feels* the reality of each part more as tension and stress are dispelled and vital-force is encouraged to flow completely within to every extremity and to enliven the body. It is useful to remember not to think, but just to watch as the body is encouraged to bend in new and different ways, personal opinions become less rigid, and mental attitudes less fixed and more open. Most of all should one observe his thoughts and become aware of the quieting effects that the *asanas* have on both the mind and body. Giving one's self totally to practice, the student will discover the joy of living life consciously, content and all right exactly where he is. There will be no need to go anywhere or prove anything, least of all to himself, for he will possess full self-acceptance and serenity right now. At such a point, he can cease his frantic pace of living and respond honestly to each new moment of life with grateful expectancy and renewed understanding.

"We are already all we will ever be. This has only to be consciously acknowledged from the soul level of awareness."
— *Roy Eugene Davis*

BEGINNING THE PRACTICE OF YOGASANAS

Hatha Yoga is composed of *Yogasanas* (which mean poses or postures), *pranayamas* (which actually mean exercises for control of life force in the body), and *mudras* (exercises which awaken vital-force in the body and are a combination of *asanas* and *pranayamas*). Some sources report that there are thousands of *asanas*, but these are really variations of certain basic poses which will be reviewed on the following pages. All of these poses are designed to beneficially influence all the muscles, nerves, glands, and bones in the body. Unlike normal exercise such as calisthenics (which work mainly on the muscle mass of the body), *Hatha Yoga asanas* have a direct effect upon the glandular and nervous system, as well as upon the muscles and circulatory system. They actually work on the body from the inside out (hence, *innercise*), affecting the most subtle side of one's nature. They encourage the glands to function efficiently and cleanse the nerve pathways. This releases heretofore untold energy in the body, as tension is dispelled with practice. Regular practice also encourages the bones of the body to line up correctly. It encourages deep relaxation and promotes good circulation throughout the body. Physical and mental problems often rapidly disappear. Almost anyone who has practiced faithfully for a few weeks will realize the value of such practice, and he will know what a difference these few daily minutes can make in his life.

The *yogis* teach that everything in the universe is composed of *prana*. This *prana* changes in frequency, from subtle to gross manifestation, so that sometimes the manifestations are visible and sometimes they are not. *Pranayamas* (*prana*—life force; *yama*—control of) are not, as is sometimes popularly stated, merely breathing exercises. The breathing is controlled while practicing *pranayamas*, but, more than that, the very life force that animates one is controlled. Thus *pranayamas* can influence very subtle areas of one's being, areas so subtle that they are seldom consciously perceived. *Pranayamas* can alter the flow of current in the body, helping one to become more stable; they can increase the flow of vital-force in the body; and they can balance the flow of energy in the body, enabling one to sit quietly and be at peace within himself.

Mudra means seal or sign. All *mudras* consist of simple body movements designed to encourage the life force to awaken in the body or to lock it in certain areas. Wherever most of the life force is concentrated in the system is where the attention will naturally be focused. Many of the more advanced *mudras* are best left to personal instruction, since they work with strong, sometimes newly awakened, energy flows in the body and a qualified personal teacher is necessary to work with them. A few of the more simple *mudras* will be discussed, however.

The *Yogasanas* are all natural movements to the body. Many derive their names from the animals who exhibit these movements, such as the Cobra, the Locust, and the Fish. The poses are not difficult; they are all easy to practice. There is no need to struggle or strain with them. When practice is first begun, the finished pose should be assumed within the mind's eye. One should see himself flowing into the pose, holding it *only* as long as it is comfortable, and then smoothly flowing out of it. It does not matter if one cannot complete the pose as perfectly as illustrated. He should simply *visualize* himself doing so. He should not be concerned with how far he is bending or even with how he looks in each pose from one day to the next. He should relax and flow in his practice, staying in the moment. Moderation should be the key, and none of the poses should cause any undue strain on the body. The body will naturally become more flexible with continued practice. Phrases such as "I can't do this one," "I'll never do it," "It's impossible for me," etc., should never be entertained in the mind. One is exactly where he should be and his body is responding exactly as it should, provided he is conscious in his practice and aware of the present moment. Then everything *is* truly in its right place.

All that is necessary is to keep the picture of the completed pose in mind, and, long before one realizes, he will be successfully completing it. But he will have enjoyed the journey along the way: getting to know himself and realizing at the same time that he has not learned all there is to know simply because he has mastered a pose. He will gain great self-confidence and will realize that life is a never-ending series of discoveries, observations, and realizations. But this will be only the beginning of his path to self-discovery and the living of life with new enthusiasm.

The basic poses should be learned first. One need not think that he must do the more difficult poses to make progress. There is great value in even the simplest of movements in *Hatha Yoga*. Every *asana* is designed to encourage the complete flow of vital-force in the body, and success will come with the quality of attention brought to the poses. One should be gentle and let the body flow without resistance, either mental or physical. He should rest between each *asana*, if necessary, to allow the heartbeat and breathing rate to return to normal, and rest also at the end of practice to allow the system time to assimilate the benefits of practice. In this way, he will not exhaust himself and will conclude his practice with more energy than he began with, since much available energy was initially tied up in stress and tension.

It is wise to keep one's daily life out of practice time. All the attention should be drawn into the space immediately surrounding one, as though this attention were contained in a protective capsule. To keep one's self centered and to remain in this present-time awareness during practice, the breath can be observed as it comes in and flows out through the nostrils, or the point between the eyebrows (called the Third Eye) can be concentrated upon (perhaps seeing a light there), or the word *OM* can be repeated silently, over and over again. This is the word from which all sounds in the universe have emerged, the initial sound of all sounds, and many people find it soothing and useful for focusing the attention. These three methods will help keep the mind off the thought process. The point of practice is *to be* where one is, totally and attentively, and these techniques can be considered tools for maintaining this awareness.

Most important to remember is to relax calmly into the postures, having no real concern with how far the body is bending. Moderation is always the guideline in all that is done, especially as the body is subjected to new and unaccustomed bending, stretching, and holding.

It is practical, even before coming to practice, to be certain that the body is in good working order. If one has a physical complaint, he should get a medical checkup. If he has a problem with his back or one centering in the skeletal system, he should see his chiropractor or osteopathic physician. Above all, one should be aware of any physical limitations and let common sense lead the way. If he has sustained a back injury, he should check with his doctor before attempting a pose which puts strain on the back, such as the Shoulder Stand, Plough, or Bow. (Many of the more simple stretching and bending movements in Hatha *Yoga*, if done slowly and smoothly, however, should be able to be practiced by almost everyone.) Doing a pose correctly means to use common sense and to be in tune with one's inner guidance. It is only when one pushes too hard or fails to use this common sense that the question of injury or overexertion arises. One must always assume final responsibility for himself. No teacher, even if he or she is standing beside a student constantly, can tell him just how far is *far enough*. He must learn to tune into his own inner guidance and always veer on the side of caution. In the beginning, a little soreness (not pain) should not be any great surprise, especially if one has not been doing regular exercise or knows when he begins that his body is a little stiff. Continuing gently will encourage this soreness and stiffness to fade gradually. And the new student will discover that this unique form of *innercise* will offer great rewards, both in improved body function and in a deeper and more meaningful inner life. In comparison with the more traditional and popular forms of exercise, *Hatha Yoga* offers the greatest benefits with the smallest possible expenditure of energy.

*"Few mortals know that
the kingdom of heaven
extends fully to this
earth plane."*
— Mahavatar Babaji

CONTINUING

The correct practice of *Yoga* will encourage positive change in one's life, and there is a basic reason for this. *Prana* (or vital-force) is the substance from which all things are formed, and gravity acts upon this vital-force, part of which is the body, exerting a downward pull on the entire system. Everyone knows the feeling, after a particularly exhausting day, of heaviness, tiredness, and of being low in energy. When one is tired, his features even appear longer and more haggard than is usual. Here is what is happening. All of the vital-force has been flowing out during the day in activity, gravity has pulled the body down, the currents in the body may be flowing very weakly and unevenly (they are being pulled down, too), and (if the body has not been cleansed or the mental attitude is negative) this vital-force may have been blocked by stress or toxins in the body, unable to reach all areas of the body and replenish the energy reserves. It is easy to understand how a person can be tired under such conditions and can look it, too.

Hatha Yoga is an ideal tonic for replenishing mind, body, and soul at such times. *Hatha Yoga* will encourage the life force to flow upwards in the body. The inverse postures will help reverse the effect of the downward flow of gravity on the body and will give a lift to all the systems. *Pranayamas* and *mudras* will help awaken life force, making it flow more strongly as it rises in the body, and, by balancing it, make the body look and be more vital and alive. Other *asanas* will encourage this life force to flow to all the extremities, releasing tension and contributing to the feeling and knowledge of health and wholeness. The resting between and at the end of postures will keep one centered within himself. And being the observer of the entire process will keep one in present-time awareness, totally here-now. Once body cleansing and diet are seen to, mental attitude will become more positive and general health will see improvement. Physical disabilities can improve and mental distractions will become less of a problem. All people should be able to live full, contented, productive lives. It is so simple to do if one will only do the things he knows he should to guarantee this. Perhaps it is so simple that many overlook the obvious. All it takes is a decision to become conscious and the discipline to follow through with the procedures. If one does the things he knows he should to succeed, he cannot possibly fail!

The new student will notice that, as his body becomes more flexible, his attitudes and opinions will likewise become less fixed and rigid. People who are very set in their ways and narrow-minded often likewise exhibit very stiff body posture and movement. Instead of being so set in his opinions, the new *Hatha* student will begin to look at life with an open attitude (if he is not already this way), no longer insisting upon his opinions and attitudes just because they are his and he has *always* felt that way, but greeting each new moment in life with an attitude of honesty and appropriateness. There is marvelous freedom in such an approach. No longer is one bound by what other people think or by what he has been taught to think traditionally, but he has total confidence in his own ability to respond suitably to life and to do it on a moment to moment basis.

A valuable lesson one quickly learns from his *Hatha* practice is that of *staying in his own space*. By this is meant minding one's own business and not interfering with other people where he has not been invited to do so. Many people get themselves into trouble when they try to offer advice to someone who does not want it or when they try to *change the world* to meet their expectations. Every person's first priority should be to get straight within his own self first. Daily practice of *Yoga* procedures will guide one on this path; there is much to learn about one's self, especially if one is totally honest and open in the process. Once one begins to trust his own intuition and inner guidance, he will be led into new situations in life, ones that will be useful to his growth. One great sage said it all so well, when asked: "What can I do to help the world?" The answer: "Mind your own business." Good advice and, for most people, not always the easiest to follow. Daily attention to the practice of awareness (*Yoga*) will guide one clearly. Knowing one's self first, one will then begin to function in life with greater clarity and understanding.

As he progresses in his practice routine, the new student will begin to understand the importance of *conserving his energy*. Most people spend tremendous amounts of energy in idle talk, gossip, and pointless activity. This energy could be directed to more useful purposes. Many people exhibit great restlessness, often staying in motion only for the purpose of being active and on the move! They find it almost impossible to sit quietly alone, even for a few moments. The physical body is formed from vital-force, and during practice one will observe that this vital-force will follow his train of thought. If it is directed towards idle use, it will be scattered uselessly. If it is directed towards positive thoughts and activity, one's life will become more productive and his vital-force will flow more strongly, giving him even more purpose and strength. He will not only have mastered the *asanas*, but, once he has seen that he himself controls this vital-force, he will be able to take control of his own life. At this point he will clearly recognize that whatever happens in his life is entirely dependent upon him, not upon other people, their opinions and actions, or any other outside influences.

A perfect example of such conservation of energy is the cat. He is a natural *yogi*. A cat is completely self-contained: not distant, but self-contained. When he relaxes, he totally relaxes, not worrying about tomorrow or yesterday. Yet he is totally in the moment. Observe how quickly he springs to life when he is suddenly aroused, with every inch of his body ready to meet and respond to the moment. He uses only as much of his energy as is necessary to accomplish his purpose (there is no tension in this fellow, worrying if he is doing something *the right way*, or guilt, worrying if he did something else the wrong way). He just lives each moment appropriately and completely.

The conscious practice of *Hatha Yoga* will lead one naturally to a more well-rounded and fulfilled life. As the *asanas* are mastered, steadiness and self-confidence (the number one ingredient for success in life) are gained. One sees how to train and discipline the mind, and he begins to observe everyday events along his way with new awareness, events and happenings he neither had time nor inclination to see before. If one fails to appreciate this very moment in his life, he will never really be able to fully appreciate the future when it arrives. He will always be thinking of what is to come after that. And when that time finally does arrive, it will hold little joy for him. His attention will already be on something else: something that will make him happy and fulfilled when *it* comes. But that something in the future never arrives. It is only by participating fully wherever one is that he can feel a real sense of unity and purpose with life.

One day, after all the practice and observations (and the time this takes will vary from student to student), one will wake up and realize that he is all right just the way he is. He may have some improvements to make, but he is basically an all right person. And life is wonderful, right where he is to participate in joyfully. It is to this meaningful moment of self-acceptance and conscious living that all the practices and disciplines will have led: when one begins to live his life consciously and fully, *making every minute count* . . . and, the nice part is, this is only the beginning!

ORDER OF PRACTICE

On the following pages, all the material that would be included at the end of a six weeks class of instruction will be explained, and a sample lesson will be detailed. The order for any lesson should be as follows: Begin with centering and attention to breathing; follow with conditioning or warm-up exercises; then *Yogasanas*; *pranayama* exercises; and finally relaxation and meditation. The *asanas* are performed in a certain order: first are the inverted postures; then backward bending; forward bending; Cobra, Locust, and Bow (usually done as a series); twisting; and perhaps a few miscellaneous poses. Practiced in this way, every muscle is systematically flexed, stretched, held, and relaxed; and every nerve and gland is encouraged to function at its peak. Maximum attention is first placed on the neck, shoulders, proceeding on down the spine into the legs, and, finally, ending with twisting to bring the body and all its systems into perfect balance.

It is not necessary to learn all of the poses at one sitting. Pick out a few and begin. But the *asanas* should be kept in the order listed, and it is useful to pick out at least one from each different grouping (forward bending, backward bending, etc.). After learning the basic movements for each of the *asanas*, allow a little variety in your routine each day. The postures can be varied, doing those you feel naturally inclined to at the moment. In this way you will remain more in tune with your body signals and will *flow* with whatever seems most appropriate at the moment. It is best to begin slowly with a few warmups, rest between poses if necessary, and always allow time at the end of practice to relax, reflect, and make the transition back to everyday living a smooth one.

CENTERING

Begin by standing relaxed and pulling all your attention into the space immediately surrounding you (this is called *centering*, bringing all your attention back inside your own self). Visualize your *space* as being contained in a bubble that completely surrounds you and eliminates any outside influences. Actually pull-in all your thoughts and feelings, either to the midpoint of the body (a point about an inch below the navel on most people), or bring the attention up to the point between the eyebrows (the *yogis* call this the Third Eye, the seat of intuition). Feel steady, calm, and entirely self-contained (*centered*) at one of these points. Accept your body lovingly, identify with it, and be relaxed, confident, mildly expectant, and at ease.

See yourself as being in tune with all your surroundings and flowing with Life. In this way you will have no problems, and the present moment is all with which you need be concerned. There is no need to be involved in thoughts; let your mind be still and quiet and your mental activity cease. Instead of thinking, become totally involved with watching your body and your breathing. Be the observer of all that occurs within your body. Watch any emotions or feelings that may surface in your mind. Do not react to them or in any way judge them if they do surface. Observe them and let them go as easily as you exhale.

Remember that you are the observer of all that occurs in your mind and body and that you are more than just your mind or body. You are a part of the One Power and One Substance that runs the Universe. And you are here to participate consciously with Life.

So first acknowledge that everything is in its right place. You are centered and at peace within yourself. You are participating joyfully in life and are totally present, here-now, in this moment. You are the witness of all that occurs from within yourself, and you can release any thoughts, feelings, or emotions that hinder this awareness simply by removing your attention from them.

To help keep yourself centered, you can watch your breath as it comes in and goes out the nostrils. (Picture the continuous inflowing and outflowing of breath through your nostrils.) Perhaps you might prefer to find a point within the body upon which to concentrate (such as the Third Eye or the heart center). Or you might want to repeat *OM* silently, over and over again (the sound from which all sounds have emerged in the universe; the primal sound). Each of these methods will focus your attention in present time and will encourage any mental activity to slow down and eventually to cease.

Become aware that your body is formed from vital-force. Get inside your body and watch this vital-force as it begins to circulate more freely. With your eyes closed, slowly raise your hands high above your head, stretching your spine as high as you are able. Bring the palms close together, but do not let them touch. Instead, be aware of the life force in your arms and hands and of the almost-magnetic pull between your hands. Slowly lower your arms to your sides, relax them, and notice how vital-force seems to pull them out and away from the body. This is *standing awareness*.

You are now in the right place at the right time, and all is well. Know this within yourself. You are entirely free in the moment, ready to observe and continue as new insights are revealed to you.

Always begin any practice session (no matter how brief) by taking a few moments to become centered. This allows you to focus your attention within your own body and your own space instead of continuously flowing outward to other people and activities. It is a time to become still and look within yourself. Without becoming overly concerned with your body, you must first learn to identify with it totally (to accept it), before you can begin to become aware of what occurs within it, much less what occurs in the mind and the more subtle spaces of your being.

Let your arms hang loosely at your sides. Relax your legs, stomach, buttocks, your entire body; be unconcerned with how you look. No one is watching, and you need to give total attention to the inner process. Be totally present, right where you are, ready to respond to the moment and to watch your thoughts, attitudes, and body responses as you begin your practice.

*"Truth must be considered to be as life-giving
as breathing itself."*
— *Sri Satya Sai Baba*

BREATHING

After becoming settled and centered within yourself, it is useful to practice a few simple breathing exercises. Most people breathe shallowly and incompletely, using only about one-third of their total lung capacity. This means that their life force probably does not flow as strongly as it could, and, since it does not thoroughly reach all the extremities in the body, full use of their vital-force and energy reserves is not available to most of them. The majority of people have no real problem with inhalation, but often they do not empty the lungs entirely each time they exhale. This means that stale air (and too much carbon dioxide) is being left in the lungs. Exhaling completely will encourage vital-force to circulate more strongly, and it will also help cleanse the lungs of any toxins brought there by the circulatory system from different areas of the body. To breathe completely is to be truly alive. When we inhale, we are breathing in life and energy; when we exhale, we are helping the body to get rid of impurities and our own vital-force and oxygen supply to circulate more completely. Use the following exercise to encourage your lungs to expel stale air and your life force to flow more completely within your system.

This is called the CLEANSING BREATH. Standing relaxed, bend over slightly and place your hands on your thighs. Make a conscious effort to breathe in sharply and fully and completely expand your lungs (taking perhaps two or three breaths), then force the air entirely out of the lungs and body, as though saying *ha*. Really concentrate on pushing the air out entirely, as though squeezing your lungs from the bottom to the top. Do this with total attention five or six times. Stand up, close your eyes, and observe the changes in your body as vital-force begins to circulate more strongly to enliven your body. At this point, since your eyes are closed, be sure to focus your attention on some inner point in space, because you may become a little dizzy, especially if you have been a habitual shallow breather or are a heavy smoker. But this dizziness will pass. Just observe it and stay centered within.

An exercise for COMPLETE BREATHING is useful after cleansing your lungs. This will encourage vital-force to flow more completely now throughout your system. There is no need to become overly concerned with how to breathe and when to breathe in *Hatha Yoga*; breathing is entirely natural to everyone. All you need to do is relax and let your body inhale when it wants and exhale when it wants. Attention should be paid, however, to breathing completely: not just deep inhalation, but breathing completely in and out in the thoracic cavity. Remember there should be no straining or abnormal movement when breathing, and you do not breathe into your belly, but deeply into your chest cavity. Visualize the lungs filling completely, from the bottom to the top, upon inhalation.Think of the lungs as containers, filling with water upon inhalation, and as toothpaste tubes, being squeezed from the bottom to the top upon exhalation. Practice COMPLETE BREATHING as follows:

Standing straight with your arms at your sides, close your eyes, and, with inhalation begin to raise your arms slowly up over your head. Stretch your entire spine and reach as high as you are able (*feel* the stretch all down your spine, as though you were suspended from a hanging bar). Having your palms up as your arms are raised indicates receptivity and openness to life. When you have inhaled completely and stretched as far as you can go, hold this position, as well as your breath, for a moment or so without strain. As you begin to exhale completely, lower your arms slowly and gracefully back to your sides. Let yourself flow in one continuous slow-motion movement. Each time you inhale, visualize breathing in light and energy. Each time you exhale, let go (with your breath) of everything that is negative and restricting in your life. Finally, stop and turn within again, observing the changes that breathing consciously and completely have made on your body. Vital-force is beginning to flow now with more strength in your entire system, and you will begin to become more aware of your whole body (especially your head and chest area).

Another exercise useful to follow at this point is the RETAINING BREATH. From a standing position, slowly raise your arms up and over your head, again stretching the spine upwards and slightly backwards. Lean forward, leading first with your head and then your arms, and retain your breath for a moment as your body relaxes and hangs forward. Stand up slowly, keeping your head tucked and uncurling your spine an inch at a time. Repeat this procedure three or four times with total attention. This exercise will encourage the life force to flow more strongly into the head and help clear the mind. Since the vital-force is also encouraged to flow more strongly to the facial area, it will improve the circulation there and promote healthy, glowing skin. This is the reason this exercise is often called the BEAUTY BREATH. It could as easily be called the MIND CLEARING BREATH.

Always follow centering with breathing exercises: remember to breathe fully and completely into your thoracic cavity and to do so with total concentration and intent. Keep your attention totally centered on what you are doing, each and every single moment.

"For where your treasure is, there will your heart be also."

— Matthew VI, 21

CONDITIONING EXERCISES

Before beginning actual practice of the *asanas*, it is a good idea to do a few conditioning or warmup exercises designed for each part of the body. This would apply especially to those who have never practiced *Yogasanas* before and who get little in the way of daily, regular exercise. Conditioning exercises actually condition each part of the body by loosening up the muscles and the joints, making the more prolonged twisting, stretching, bending, and holding that is to follow in the *asanas* much easier on the system. They can help release some of the physical kinks the body acquires from tension, making the *asanas* much easier to concentrate fully upon and to relax into. They can be extremely helpful for older people just beginning practice or for anyone recovering from a long illness or injury as a test of endurance and general health. They can also be useful as a quick way to spot any weak or very tight areas in the body which might bear a little extra attention.

From day to day the body will vary in its degree of stiffness and tightness, and a few warmups done slowly and thoughtfully at the beginning of practice can help you become aware of just how limber you are at the moment and what areas in your body you might want to concentrate upon. Do not overlook warmups because they look too easy. Many of these exercises are adaptations of classic *Yoga* poses, and there is value to the body in even the simplest of movements. Each exercise encourages the more complete flow of vital-force, especially to the body part being concentrated upon.

As you continue to practice and your body becomes more accustomed to the bending and stretching of the *Yogasanas*, you may find all of the warmups to be unnecessary. On such occasions, you might want to begin with the Sun Salutation, which works on every part of the body simultaneously in one series of movements. On other occasions, you might want to use all the warmups, certain ones, or intersperse them between the postures. You can repeat any of them between postures if there is need to do so: the Neck Roll, for instance, can help relieve any tension accumulated in the neck area between the poses. After you have learned the warmups and how to tune into your body needs and signals, use the exercises in your practice whenever they *feel* necessary. But use them fairly regularly until your body has become conditioned to practice, for they can be most helpful in setting the stage for the *asanas* to follow. The exercises here described begin, as will the *asanas*, with concentration first in the head and neck area, continuing on down the spine to the feet, concluding with twisting and general body flexibility.

FOR THE NECK: One of the simplest and most effective exercises that can be done for the neck is the NECK ROLL. A strong, supple, and limber neck is vital in the performance of all the *asanas*, and it is useful to release tension from this area so that vital-force can flow unimpeded into the head and brain, helping to clear the mind and therin relax the body. Much of the tension accrued in everyday living eventually settles in the neck and shoulder area. Practicing this easy exercise can help prevent headaches and the up-tight feelings that result from tension and stress. The NECK ROLL can be done any time during the day when you become aware of tightness in the neck area. Use it often.

While in a standing position, close your eyes and drop your chin forward to rest on your chest (or as close as you are able to bring it). Begin to rotate your head slowly to the left. Visualize your left ear touching your left shoulder. It does not matter whether it actually does or not. Visualize it and let it go at that. Continue to rotate your head as far back as comfortable, never straining; rotate on to the right (again visualizing your right ear touching your right shoulder); and bring your chin back to your chest (or as close as possible). Be aware of any cracking and popping sounds in your neck. Now reverse and go in a clockwise direction. Imagine that your neck is on a greased ball-bearing and let it slide with no resistance. Do this slowly and intently two or three times in each direction. (A variation is to bring your arms up to shoulder level, with your wrists flexed upwards for a little extra pull, and proceed as before.) Finally, place your hands on your neck and turn your neck far to the right, to the left, and in any direction that feels good to get rid of any extra kinks left there. Always proceed smoothly and gently. Continue rotating your neck until all the noises have ceased and it feels totally relaxed. Close your eyes and observe any changes in the flow of life force in your body due to this exercise (especially in your neck and shoulder area). Feel the warmth in this part of your body that is this vital-force.

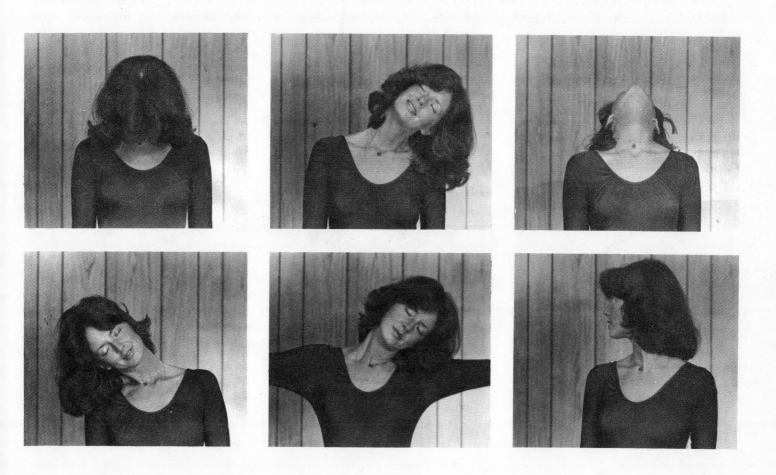

41

FOR THE SHOULDER AREA: **An exercise called THE BLADE to limber the entire shoulder area can be done next. First raise your arms to shoulder level, wrists flexed, and imagine that you are pressing a coin between your shoulder blades. Perhaps you might close your eyes to concentrate better. Keep your arms level and still and move only your shoulder blades. This will massage your shoulders and loosen all the muscles and joints in that area. Do this four or five times; close your eyes, stay relaxed, and note the increased warmth from the flow of vital-force now from your shoulders down to the tingling in your fingertips.**

You can also ROTATE THE SHOULDER AREA to help loosen it up. With your arms at shoulder level, rotate your hands, arms, and shoulder blades as far forward as possible; hold, and rotate as far back as possible. Try to make your shoulders do a 360 degree turn. Let them roll smoothly, with no forcing or jerking. Close your eyes, and, once again, be the observer of further changes in your body. Always observing the changes in your body as you progress will keep you in present-time awareness.

FOR THE CHEST AND THE LUNGS: Standing erect, slowly and deliberately raise your arms out in front of your body. Keep your wrists flexed. Bring your arms back at shoulder level and continue until your fingers can be clasped behind your back. Look up (keeping your forehead relaxed) while leaning slightly backwards and raise your arms out away from your body and towards the ceiling. Gently lean forward, bending from the waist and hip area, and bring your arms high into the air over your body. Hold for a moment; feel the stretch; stand up slowly, keeping your head tucked and uncurling your spine an inch at a time. Take a complete breath and relax. Do this three times, always taking time to turn within at the last to observe the further flow of vital-force in your body. This pose is called the CHEST LIFT and is actually an *asana* which encourages the lungs to empty all the stale air with each breath, massages the shoulders and back area, and encourages life force to flow more strongly to the upper parts of the body. With this *asana* you will actually be able to *feel* the upper part of your body more fully and completely.

FOR THE UPPER TORSO: **To limber the upper torso and stretch the entire spine, stand with your legs about two feet apart and clasp your hands in front of your body. Reach up high over your head and bend slightly backwards. Swing forward gently and let your upper torso swing down between your legs, with your arms continuing to swing back and forth until they come to a stop on their own. Visualize CHOPPING WOOD with an ax. This exercise will loosen up the entire spine and encourage flexibility. Do this two or three times. Always remember to pause and look inside your body to note further changes occurring in the flow of vital-force. What parts of your body are you now more aware of?**

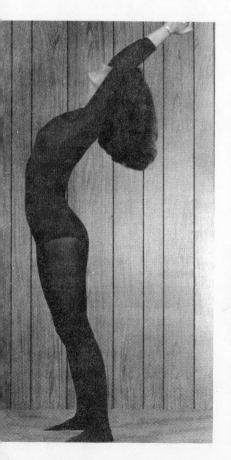  

To encourage flexibility of the spine and legs and to strengthen the back, you can do the PENDULUM. Stand with your legs about three feet apart and hang from your waist, letting your arms drape down comfortably. Begin to swing your body and arms from side to side, as though your arms were the pendulum of a grandfather clock. Continue to swing in this manner for a few moments, then stop your body and let your arms come to rest on their own. *Hang* in this position for a short time, with your eyes closed and attention turned within. This position is most useful for strengthening the back, especially the lower back, and the swinging to and fro encourages general flexibility and coordination.

TWISTING THE TORSO: **A useful exercise for TWISTING the trunk and upper torso can follow next. Stand and raise your arms to shoulder level, wrists flexed upwards. Keeping your arms and shoulders level, gently twist your upper body as far to the right as possible; hold; reverse to the left. Pivot on your left foot (then right foot) and let the upper torso do most of the twisting. Twisting increases flexibility of the spine and gives a unique turn to the spine and trunk of the body not found in regular stretching and bending. Twist smoothly and easily three times to the right and three times to the left, pausing at last, with total intent, to observe the further awakened life force which animates your body.**

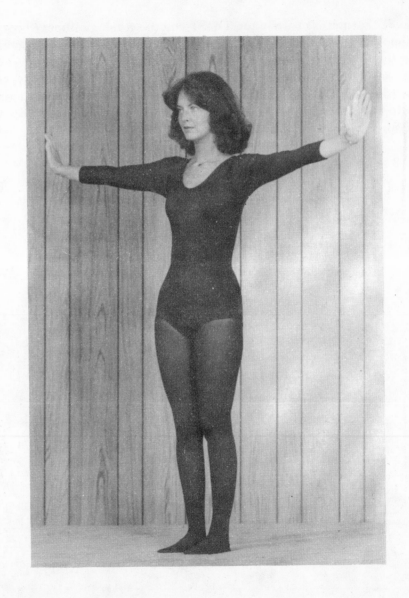

KNEE BENDS: You will find KNEE BENDS useful for limbering your legs and knees. Stand relaxed, raising your arms to shoulder level (or placing your palms together over your head) and slowly bend your legs, lowering your body until all the weight is on the balls of your feet with the buttocks and lower legs touching. Without pausing, continue smoothly back up to the standing position in one continuous flowing movement. This can be done five or six times. The last time down, stop and balance for a moment or two. To help maintain your balance, fix your attention on a point in front of you (either on the wall or on the floor a few feet in front of you) and allow your thoughts to cease completely. *Just be.* Stand up again, pause, and note any further changes in your body. Really get inside your body and identify with the warmth and energy you feel. Accept your body lovingly.

FOR THE ANKLES: Be sure to pay attention to the ankles, one of the first parts of the body to stiffen and show signs of age. Simple foot rotations can be done (lifting your leg, pointing your toe, and making circles with your foot), or you can do an exercise which resembles skiing. With your feet and legs together, swing your hips to the right; let your arms, upper body, and feet swing to the left (as you might look on a downhill turn when skiing). Reverse, swinging your hips to the left, and your arms, upper torso, and feet to the right. Do this three times on each side of your body and you will notice that stiffness in the ankles will begin to disappear. Limber ankles are a necessity in the *asanas*, especially in all of the sitting postures. Remember to proceed smoothly and easily, never applying too much pressure to any part of the body to *force* it to bend. Always visualize the pose you wish to assume and allow your body to *flow* into it.

FOR THE FEET: The feet should not be neglected when warming up the body. A simple exercise here to encourage vital-force to flow more strongly and unhindered is as follows. With your feet together, rise up onto the tiptoes and balls of your feet. Begin to roll both feet outwards (using your arms to balance); come back onto your heels; roll to the insides of your feet (at this point try to bring your thighs together); and come back onto the balls of your feet. Do this at least three or four times. You may notice cracking noises in the feet and ankles similar to those you heard in the neck during the Neck Roll. Finally, stop and fully identify with the warmth and vital-force now flowing more strongly into your feet.

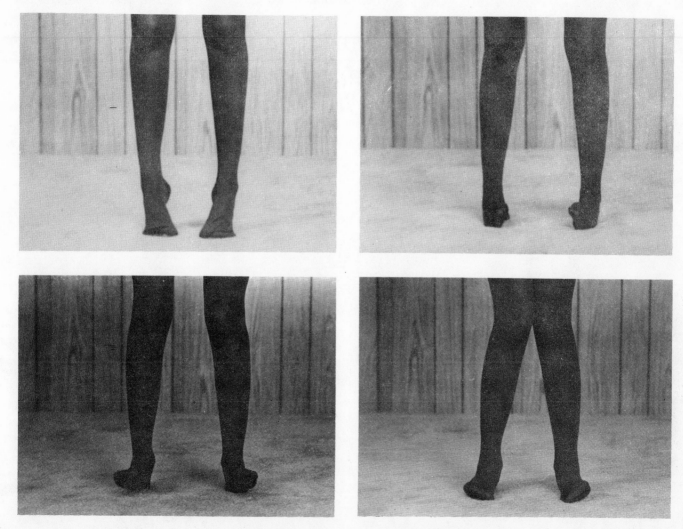

*From Pure Joy springs all creation;
by Joy it is sustained, towards Joy it
proceeds and to Joy it returns.*

FOR THE BACK: **To perform this exercise, kneel down on your hands and knees. Stretch upwards and arch your back (visualize a frightened cat), placing your head between your arms and looking up at your stomach. Hold this position for a moment; look up at the ceiling and slowly sway your back down towards the floor. Let your body flow from one movement to the next, repeating the entire exercise three or four times. Finally, lower your chest as close to the floor as possible in an extreme stretch, without touching your chin to the floor. This movement will give you a clue as to how perfect your posture is at the present time. The harder it is to touch your chest to the floor, the more improvement your posture can stand. The STRETCHING CAT will help strengthen the back and make it more flexible. It will also improve body posture and encourage vital-force to flow strongly to the reproductive organs to strengthen them. Pause again after completing this exercise and be the totally involved observer of the further changes that have occurred in your body.**

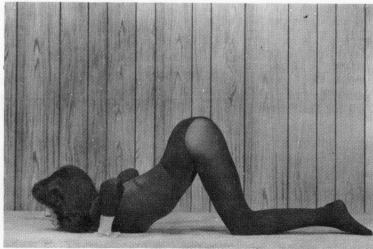

FOR THE STOMACH: Lie now on your back. Place your attention on your abdominal muscles and use them to gently lift your right leg up as nearly vertical as possible. Relax your leg, letting the abdominal muscles do the work. Hold for a moment; lower your leg slowly back to the floor; lift your left leg and lower it in the same manner; finally lift and lower both legs together. This exercise will encourage the blood to return to the heart and is a good nerve stabilizer (helps purify the nerves by encouraging the flow of vital-force to increase through them). Close your eyes and identify with this vital-force, which forms your body and *is* your body.

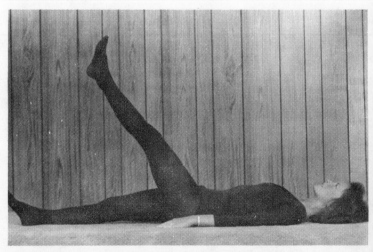

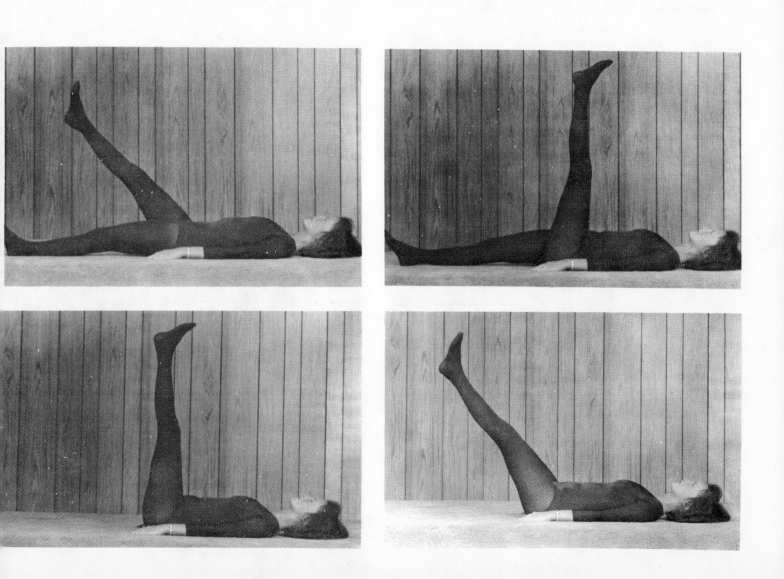

A conditioning exercise useful for helping remove excess fat from the hips, thighs, and abdomen is the WALK. Lie on your back; raise both legs vertically and walk with your feet in the air, keeping them flexed towards your face. Try to keep your legs as straight as possible and walk very gently. Continue to walk in this manner as long as comfortable, being careful not to overdo, especially if your lower back is weak or you are an older person just beginning practice. Lower your legs smoothly (using the abdominal muscles) and with control back to the floor. Again, close your eyes; turn within and observe the flow of *prana* throughout your system.

 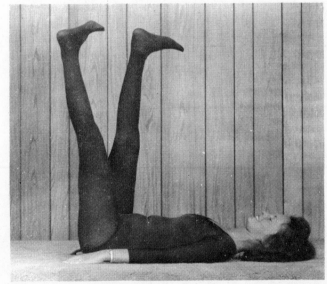

TWISTING THE ENTIRE TORSO: Remaining on your back, place your arms at shoulder level, and, bending both legs, lift them up, coming as close to your chest as possible. Turn your head to the right, twist your body and legs to the left, touching your legs to the floor if possible. (Remember to visualize completing the pose and not be overly concerned with how your body is responding.) Keep your shoulders and arms on the floor throughout the twisting: this will give you a much more effective and complete twist. Twist gently three times in each direction. Lower your legs back to the floor; close your eyes and feel the strong flow of life force now through your shoulders, spine and legs.

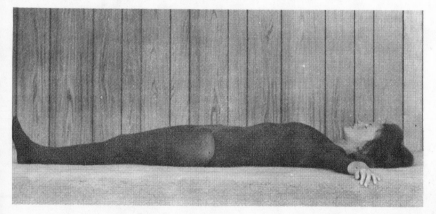

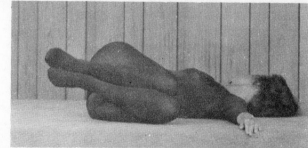

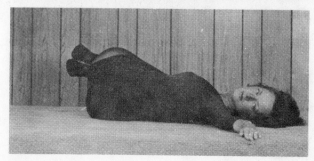

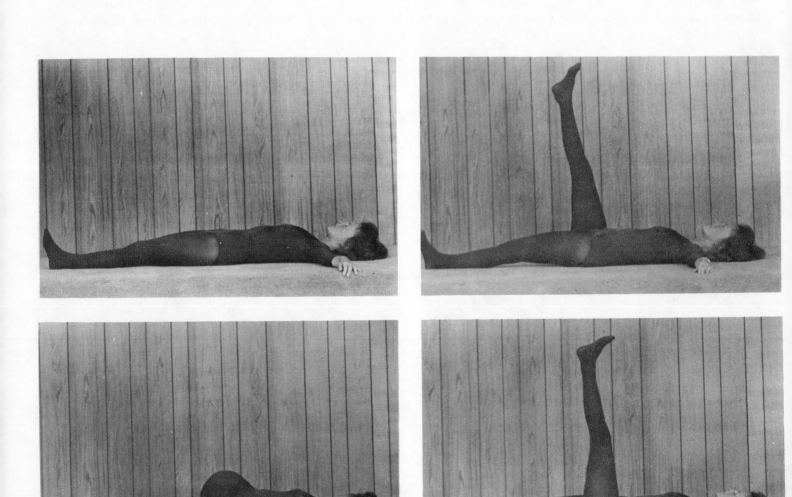

A variation of this exercise is to lift your right leg in the air, twist your head to the right, and, keeping your shoulders and body as still as possible, swing your right leg over the left side of your body, coming as close to the floor with your foot as you are able. Keep the left leg flat on the floor. Do the opposite with your left leg: head to the left, shoulders and body flat on the floor, bringing the left leg over the right side of your body, touching the foot to the floor if possible, right leg flat on the floor. Do this at least twice with both legs. This exercise affords an excellent twisting effect to the body. Always finish on one side of the body whatever you do for the other. This encourages vital-force to flow evenly in a more balanced manner and harmonizes all the sytems in your body. Close your eyes and *look* inside your body. *Feel*, identify with, and accept your body in its entirety.

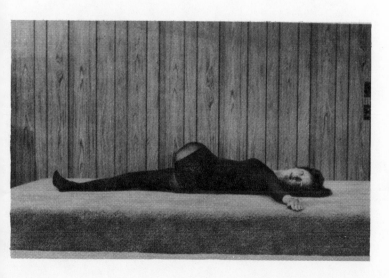

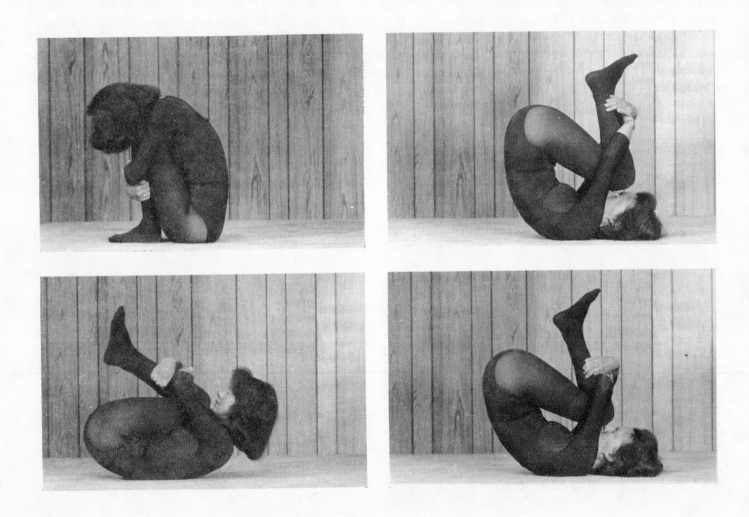

ROCKING: **A useful way to conclude your warmup session is to massage the spine and help relax your body by ROCKING on your spine. Curl up into a ball, hold your ankles, and let your body rock to and fro on your spine a dozen or so times. You can curl up tightly or loosely, whichever is more natural and comfortable. A variation is to cross your ankles, clasp your toes, bring your forehead forward to touch the toes and floor, and rock gently back. After rocking back, extend your legs (while still holding the toes), and touch the toes to the floor behind your head (or come as close as you are able). Rock very gently, with a regular flowing rhythm. Feel the spine begin to relax. Be careful of rocking too far back on your neck if you have had any recent or long-time neck injury. Tune into your body. Get inside it and totally identify with it and with the vital-force which animates it. Learn to watch this life force and soon you will realize how easy it is to direct it. After you have finished rocking, lie down on the floor for a few minutes and relax in the following *asana*.**

THE CORPSE POSE (*SAVASANA*)

Lie quietly on your back now and allow yourself to relax completely in the *asana* known as the Corpse Pose; *Savasana* is its Sanskrit name. Stretch your entire spine out on the floor (make sure your neck is on the floor and that there is no strain on the lower back); spread your legs and extend your arms out from your sides (palms up, once again, for receptivity); turn your head from side to side until it rests comfortably on the floor. No part of the body should be touching another. Close your eyes, turn within, and become very aware of all the vital-force within, which is your body. Be aware of your heartbeat and breathing and remain in this posture until your heartbeat and breathing rate have returned to normal. This gives your body time to assimilate the benefits of all the warmups you have just done and allows your energy and attention to remain totally centered within your own being. This is the time to be still, to get in tune with your body and your real Self, and to accept both totally and lovingly.

Watch the thought processes in your mind. If any thoughts do come, look at them honestly and let them go. Do not try to stop them. Trying will actually encourage them more. Surrender to Life and this very moment. Watch your thoughts without judgment and release them completely as you exhale. All this takes is a conscious decision and follow-through: doing and not trying. Remember to watch your breath (or whatever method you have chosen to focus your attention) to keep yourself centered and your attention off your thoughts. If you find some of your inner thoughts disturbing, you can remind yourself that you are not those thoughts. They are only mental images with no reality of their own. You are not your thoughts, feelings, or attitudes, and, realizing this, you can begin to take control of your own life. Your life force will follow your train of thought: wherever you direct your attention is where most of your vital-force will be concentrated. If your attention is focused upon anything disturbing, negative, or non-useful, withdraw that attention, and the vital-force will withdraw, taking all of the energy away from the thoughts.

Savasana is excellent for placing one in the witness state: giving him time to be quiet and observe all the thoughts and feelings that he calls himself, but which, in Reality, is only his restless mind. When the vital-force in the body is slowed down, as it is in this posture, the thought processes also become more subtle, and here is the opportunity to observe the more subtle internal processes, as well as to inquire as to just *who* and *what* one really is. Revealing insights can come at such relaxed and surrendered moments.

Savasana affords complete relaxation to every part of the body. The *yogis* call this *asana* conscious sleep, and it can often be more refreshing to the body and mind than actual sleep. Many times one takes tension, worry, guilt, and frustration into his sleep hours with him. This can prevent the body from relaxing totally and the sleep hours from giving him total refreshment. But, in the Corpse Pose, one is *consciously* relaxing the body and mind first, getting rid of any tension there and releasing non-useful mental images, so that the time spent in this posture is most healing and restful to the entire system.

You can remain in this pose for a few minutes any time during the day whenever you feel tired or stressed. It can be a most useful and sensible way to spend a little time consciously.

*"I have learned, in whatever state
I am, therewith to be content."*
— Philippians IV, II

THE SUN GREETING (*SURYANAMASKAR*)

After having practiced for some time, you may wish to substitute the Sun Greeting for the previous conditioning exercises. The Sun Greeting is one complete series of warmups that works on all parts of the body at once. It is sometimes called SALUTATION TO THE SUN. This is an *asana* of twelve continuous poses performed as one series of movements: six poses to get the body down onto the floor and the same six done in reverse order to bring the body back to its original starting position. Many people find this pose very energizing, a useful way to get the vital-force in the body flowing very quickly before practice. It can also be most relaxing for the body if done several times rather quickly. The Sun Greeting was traditionally performed at dawn to greet the morning sun: source of power, energy, and light for the earth. When you perform this *asana*, visualize all of the vital-force in your body radiating from the heart center (the point near the middle of the chest near the location of the heart) and visualize the light and energy from the sun entering your body there, energizing and centering you in your heart center.

1. Stand erect, feet together. Bring your palms to the heart center in the traditional form of Hindu greeting. This is a *mudra* called the Salutation Seal, and it encourages the awakening of life force in your heart center.
2. Slowly raise your arms high upwards and backwards over your head, keeping your thumbs locked together. Bend your body backwards slightly and look back towards your hands. Relax your face.
3. Bend forward slowly, leading first with your head, and place your hands on the floor on the outsides of your feet, keeping your legs as straight as possible and your head as close to your knees as possible. Once your hands and feet are placed in this position, they should not move forwards or backwards during subsequent positions; experiment to find the correct placement to allow for this.

4. Extend your left leg back, resting on your left knee, the ball of the left foot, and your right foot. Come up onto your fingertips, with your right leg pressed into your chest, and gaze without strain upwards toward the ceiling.
5. Slide your right leg back even with the left, straighten both legs, and try to flatten both feet on the floor. Your body should assume the position of an inverted V. Place your hands flat on the floor and put your head between your arms, gazing up at your stomach.
6. Without moving your hands, bring your body back to assume a kneeling position on both ankles. Keeping your hands stationary on the floor, slowly begin to slide your entire body onto the floor from this kneeling position. Lead with your forehead, then slide your chest and stomach gently along the floor.
7. Arch your head, neck, and chest up off the floor in a rather extreme stretch. Keep your palms flat on the floor. Look up at the ceiling without strain or wrinkling the forehead. Your elbows will be bent slightly.
8. Turn your toes under, straighten your arms and legs, and begin to raise your body back into the inverted V position. Place your head between your arms and look up at your abdomen. Make this one continuous movement.

9. Thrust your left leg forward, coming to rest against your chest and between your hands on the floor. Gaze skyward, keeping your forehead relaxed.

10. Slide your right leg forward to rest alongside the left, with your legs as straight as possible and your head close to your knees (touching, if possible).

11. Stand up smoothly, bringing your arms up over your head, bending slightly backwards and gazing back towards your hands.

12. Stand erect once more, palms together at your heart center.

Although it may take some time to learn all the movements in this Greeting, it should be visualized as one continuous, flowing movement, so that there is no discernible break between one position and the next. A little practice will help it flow smoothly. Any of the positions may also be used separately as warmups for a particular part of the body, if you so desire.

Learn one pose at a time and visualize yourself flowing gently through each one. Do as many greetings as you feel inclined. A few will energize the body, and more will tend to tire the body somewhat and help it relax at the end of a busy day. Do not be in a hurry with the Sun Greeting. Learn it thoroughly and be positive that it can be learned perfectly. This means watching your attitudes in the process of learning (never giving in to negativity). Visualize yourself doing the poses smoothly and correctly and give yourself time to make this a reality.

If you are using the Sun Greeting as a warmup for the body, stop and relax for a few moments in the Corpse Pose before going on to the *asanas*.

"As he thinketh in his heart, so is he."
— Proverbs, XXIII, 5

ASANAS

Now you can begin the actual practice of the *Yogasanas. Asana* is a Sanskrit word which means *to hold motionless* (Sanskrit being one of our oldest known languages, in which every letter carries the original intent of its meaning). Each of the poses has a Sanskrit name which will be listed along with the more familiar name on the following pages. The *asanas* are composed of three types of movements: bending, stretching, and twisting; but it is to the holding motionless and steady that our practice leads us. At such time, all the currents in the body will be balanced, everything will be in perfect evenness, and we will experience the oneness of mind, body, and soul. The bending and stretching movements help the body to get rid of tension; twisting affords a unique twist to the spine and internal organs; holding motionless helps build self-confidence, discipline, and strength of character. There will also be subtle effects upon the mind which can lead to a more fulfilled and satisfying way of life. All of the poses contribute to strength, endurance, vitality, serenity of mind, and order and purpose in living. It does not matter whether one is six or sixty; *Yoga* is for all ages and all people.

It is best to approach your practice time in a calm, meditative mood, with an open frame of mind and a feeling of expectancy. The most useful way to practice is simply *to be* in the moment, totally present, observing everyting that occurs objectively. Try not to *think* about anything; instead, keep yourself settled in the moment by watching the breath come in and out the nostrils (or repeating Om silently, or concentrating on the Third Eye Center). Do whatever feels natural for you. If you should find thoughts flickering in your mind, observe them with no judgment and let them go completely. Focus your attention in whatever manner you choose, and soon your mind will settle down and your thoughts will become more subtle, sometimes ceasing entirely.

Learn the mechanics of a pose first; then visualize, in your mind's eye, how the completed pose would look. Close your eyes and let your body flow into the pose; hold it as long as it is comfortable; flow out of it. Begin slowly and with conscious intent. Always give yourself time to learn to execute the *asanas* with precision. Do not judge yourself at any stage of practice. Let your body flow and sink into the poses, which are all natural movements to the body. Be gentle with your body; not forcing or straining helps your body to relax into a pose. Flow into the pose and hold it *only* as long as common sense dictates. Moderation should always be your guideline. Once you have practiced for some time, holding the pose motionless will occur naturally. Until then, practice each posture three or four times, flowing in and out, without being in a hurry. Be conscious of what is happening in your body: the changes from one pose to the next, a sudden awareness of a certain part of your body, and any emotions or attitudes surfacing in your mind during these changes. Each of the *asanas* should be performed with self-control and gracefulness. Do not allow your body to collapse from a pose. Each one should be completed with full attention and total self-containment and control. For this to occur, you must remain in your own space, with your attention centered entirely within your own being and in the present moment.

Use only the energy needed to complete a pose. This means not wasting your vital-force in idle thoughts (daydreaming or negative thoughts) or needless body movements. Utilize only the muscles necessary to perform a pose; let every other muscle and body part relax completely. Pay special attention not to wrinkle your forehead; this muscle is usually the first one to register body tension and can tie up much of your life force needlessly. Complete the posture in one continuous movement. Realize that the way your body is responding is exactly right for you. Make no comparisons or judgments on any basis. Relax and enjoy the fullness of the moment; be totally involved in it.

Always complete a pose that is begun on the right side of your body with the identical movement on the left side of your body. The idea is to bring everything into harmony and balance, and treating both sides of your body identically will encourage this balance. Most people will discover that their body is tighter on one side than the other. This means that vital-force is impeded there for some reason and the available energy reserves are diminished. This could be due to tension or the need for body cleansing. Seeing to correct diet, body cleansing, and daily performance of the *asanas* will encourage this life force to flow more completely into the blocked areas. The nerve pathways will be cleansed, and vital-force will then be able to flow unhindered. As you tune in with your body, if you should notice any particularly tight areas, think of these areas as blocked energy (vital-force) and visualize sending your breath to these areas, thus allowing them to relax and your body to sink more deeply and comfortably into the pose. Never fight or struggle with body tightness since your muscles will only resist with more tension. Flow into your movements gently and think of sending any tightness away with each exhalation of your breath. Sometimes, during the course of practice, air may escape through various body openings. This is an entirely natural process and should be thought of in this way. It occurs often in any *Hatha Yoga* class and should be no cause of embarrassment to anyone.

Do not be concerned with physical progress in your practice; it will be natural and forthcoming. Do not become involved in a game of comparison: how far your body bent yesterday and how far it might bend today. Do not think about the future and what you wish to accomplish next week. This always takes you out of present time and focuses your attention on goals, instead of keeping you in the *now*. (Sometimes you may find it necessary to apply conscious will power to make these decisions and stick with them.) The Zen Masters say that all that matters is *now*. Make your practice time the time, for you alone, to get to know yourself: who you *really* are and what motivates you. The answers that surface can be quite enlightening. Do this by remaining constantly aware of all that happens in your body and mind during practice. Remain the objective observer of all that occurs, and this objectivity will be carried over into everyday living, allowing you to live as a conscious person does: content, serene, and self-contained. Stay completely present in this time and space, watching any emotions and attitudes, as well as *tuning in completely* with all parts of your body and *feeling* it from the inside out, every step of the way.

Allow ample time to rest between postures (such as in the Corpse Pose), so that your body can assimilate the benefits of each pose, your heartbeat and breathing can return to normal, and the inner processes can be fully observed. Be conscious of remaining in present time and be conscious of any thoughts surfacing in your mind, especially at these quiet times. Practice daily and with purpose, guided by common sense and gentleness. Let your practice lead you into an awareness of what it is like to live life making every moment count. The correct practice of *Yogasanas* can result in the complete sense of oneness with all life, with total appropriateness in the moment, and we are wise to make the most of this opportunity.

"I have everything, yet have nothing; and although I possess nothing, still of nothing am I in want."
— *Terence*

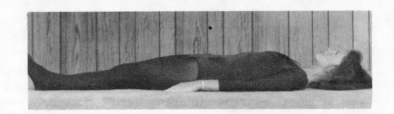

THE SHOULDER STAND (*SARVANGASANA*)

Begin lying down on your back, with your entire spine (including your neck) stretched out on the floor. Bend the chin down towards the chest. Your arms should be at your sides with your legs extended together.

Using the abdominal muscles only, slowly raise your legs up off the floor and continue to bring them back over your head, letting the trunk of your body follow. (Beginners may rock into this position at first, if they lack initial strength to lift the trunk and legs from a prone position.) Place your hands at your waist and hip area, supporting your body, and straighten your legs over your hips. Your chin should press into your chest, and all the muscles not required for this *asana* should be relaxed. This is the Half-Shoulder Stand. Close your eyes and visualize breathing deeply from the bottom of your lungs.

As your back strengthens, it can be straightened by bringing your hands up the back towards the shoulder blades. Your chin will now be pressed tightly into your chest. Your forehead, legs, buttocks, and abdominal muscles will be relaxed. *Sink* into the pose. Visualize your body as straight as a plumb line, from the toes down through your shoulders. Your toes should be over your eyes and your feet relaxed (toes not pointed). Breathing will seem constricted to the lower part of the chest. Feel the oneness in your entire body; be aware of the vital-force within. This is the Full Shoulder Stand.

Hold either of these poses only as long as comfortable. To come out of each pose, slowly lower your knees to your forehead. Gently place your arms back on the floor, and, keeping your head and neck flat on the floor, press into your arms and uncurl your spine, placing it back on the floor one vertebra at a time. When your spine is fully on the floor again, straighten your legs and use your abdominal muscles to lower your legs back to the floor. Come out of the pose gracefully and entirely self-contained. Close your eyes and rest in *Savasana*. Be aware of the awakened life force within your body and realize that this vital-force *is* your body.

When your back is fully strengthened, the pose may be completed as follows: with arms placed back on the floor, slowly lower your trunk to the floor from the inverted position, keeping your legs straight and a little back over your head. Uncurl your spine, keeping your legs as close to your forehead as possible. When the trunk is fully on the floor again, straighten your legs and lower them to the floor with control, as before.

A variation on the Shoulder Stand, after it can be held motionless for some time, is as follows: from the inverted position, allow gravity to lower your right leg to the floor behind your head (or as close as you can come to the floor without forcing); hold and raise it up again slowly. Repeat with your left leg and then with both legs. You can also lower your legs, spread them as far apart as possible, and twist the trunk of your body gently to the right and left.

The Shoulder Stand, *Sarvangasana*, is an inverse posture often referred to as the *all body posture*. It affects literally every part of the body at once. It stimulates and regulates the thyroid gland, which controls and regulates body metabolism, thereby tending to normalize body weight. It reverses the flow of gravity on the body, encouraging *prana* to flow upwards in the body and relieving pressure on all the organs; improves general circulation; strengthens the neck and shoulders; clears the mind; makes the eyes brighter, the skin clearer, and encourages the healthy growth of hair; and refreshes the body and mind by reversing the magnetic pull of the earth's North and South poles. Holding the pose motionless will result in the slipping away of tension and fatigue, and the central nervous system will be refined by the increased flow of vital-force throughout the body.

THE EASY BRIDGE AND THE FULL BRIDGE (*SETHU BANDHASANA*)

To relieve any stress in your lower back area following the Shoulder Stand, follow with the Easy Bridge. Lying on the floor, bend your legs and bring both heels of your feet close to your buttocks. Arms should remain on the floor alongside your body. Lift the trunk of your body up off the floor, forming a bridge with it. Hold and repeat this two or three times. A few neck rolls can also be done to relieve any stress in the neck following the extreme bending in the Shoulder Stand.

For more advanced practitioners, the Full Bridge can be practiced as a variation from the Shoulder Stand. While in the full Shoulder Stand, support your body weight with your wrists placed at the waist area on your hips (experiment to find the most comfortable placement: wrists forwards or backwards on the hips). Bring your legs back slightly over your head and spread your legs, as if in a running position, your left leg far back over your head and your right one forward of your body. Allow your right leg to swing down forward towards the floor, with the left leg and trunk of the body following. Lower your legs slowly, with control, and do not allow them to drop heavily.

Keeping your feet together, arch the trunk of your body (as though it were a bridge), and slide your feet out away from your buttocks, making your legs become straighter. Support your body firmly with your elbows and wrists.

Hold; bring your feet back towards your buttocks; push lightly up off the floor with both feet and swing your right leg back to its vertical postion, following with the left leg. Repeat, leading this time with your left leg. Remain in total control of your entire body. Come out of the posture exactly as you did in the Shoulder Stand.

Common sense should be exercised, especially in this pose, not to push your body too fast or too far, even if you are very supple and limber. Get inside your body and totally identify with it as all the stretching and bending are accomplished. Then rest in *Savasana* for a sufficient amount of time to bring your body processes back to normal.

Both of the Bridge poses allow the body to stretch in the opposite direction from the Shoulder Stand, thus completing the stretch in both directions and relieving stress. They also strengthen the abdominal muscles and the wrists.

THE PLOUGH (*HALASANA*)

Lie on your back with your arms at your sides and your legs together.

Gradually raise your legs and the trunk of your body up and back over your head as you did in the Shoulder Stand. (Remember to use your abdominal muscles to raise your legs.) Continue to bring your hips back over your head, palms pressed to the floor, until your toes touch the floor behind your head. Do not jerk or strain; visualize your body flowing smoothly with no resistance. Now bring your arms back to touch your toes, which are curled under towards your head, giving an extra pull on the hamstring muscles of the legs. Keep your legs as straight as possible. Breathing will be concentrated in the thoracic area of the chest, and the chin will be pressed tightly into the chest. Think of sending your breath to any areas of resistance.

As proficiency is gained in this posture, variations can be added. Raise your arms straight in the air and an increase in the flow of vital-force to your head area will be encouraged. Spread your legs as far apart as possible, once in the Plough position, and press your ankles gently towards the floor. Hold; bring your legs together again; gently lower your knees to the floor, if possible, on either side of your ears. To accomplish this, first make sure that your hips are bent as far back over your head as possible. Your arms should remain on the floor, and the position should be held only as long as it is comfortable. This is the Ear-to-Knee Pose.

To complete the Plough pose, slowly bring your knees to your forehead and uncurl your spine bit by bit as in the Shoulder Stand. Relax completely.

The Plough is so named because of the resemblance of the body to the ancient plough of India when the pose is completed. It increases the flexibility of the hips, legs, and spine. Often called the Hang-Over Pose, it helps clear the mind by encouraging life force to circulate in greater volume to the head. It strengthens the voice and the eyes, and it tones the abdominal muscles and encourages the thyroid gland to function efficiently. If held motionless, fatigue will disappear and the nervous system will be rejuvenated.

THE POSE OF A CHILD (*VAJRASANA VARIATION*)

Kneeling on your feet and legs with your body stretched forward, turn your head to one side, keeping your arms stretched alongside your body; relax. Your arms may also be stretched out in front as an extension of your body. In this position, feel as though someone were pulling your arms, stretching your spine out completely to its entire length. Be aware of your heartbeat and breathing and changes now occurring in your body.

The Pose of A Child, along with the Corpse Pose, is another relaxation posture. If used for relaxation after a pose such as the Plough, it stretches the body in the opposite direction, completing the stretch in both directions and allowing the body to relax totally. It can be used any time you wish to rest between postures or by itself.

THE FISH (*MATSYASANA*)

Lie on your back, spine stretched completely out on the floor, arms at your sides, and legs together. Relax and take a few complete breaths. Slip your hands just under the sides of your upper thighs, transfer your body weight to your elbows and buttocks, and arch your back up off the floor. Place the crown of your head flat on the floor, so that your throat is stretched completely open. Part of your body weight will now be borne by your head. Relax your forehead and your chin (smile slightly) while gazing backwards. Your chest will be thrown open and your breathing should be concentrated in the thoracic cavity. Gently slide your hands out from under your thighs and place them on top of your thighs (arms stretched out completely). This is the Beginning Fish. You can stretch your arms back over your head and hold them there for a short time to be certain that weight is properly distributed on your body in this pose.

To complete the pose, slide your hands back under your thighs, transfer your weight back to your elbows and buttocks, and lift (do not slide) your head from the floor, straightening your spine and lying completely stretched out on the floor again. Relax completely; flow in and out of the pose several times.

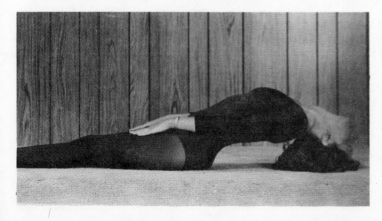

If you are an advanced student, you may begin by sitting in the Lotus Posture (see Sitting Postures). Lean backwards on one elbow at a time.

Place the crown of your head on the floor, arch your back upwards, and place your hands on your feet (hold your toes). Hold this position only as long as comfortable; then, transferring your weight back to your elbows and buttocks, return to the sitting position. Straighten your legs, lie down quietly, and observe the changes within your system.

Some *Hatha Yogis* are able to float in water for a length of time in this posture, their bodies resembling fish, which is why the pose is called the Fish. *Matsyasana* stretches the lungs, bathes them in vital-force, and discourages respiratory problems such as asthma and shortness of breath. If done following the Shoulder Stand, it counterstretches the neck, relieving any stress caused there by the Shoulder Stand. It strengthens the spine and aids in improving posture, and, since vital-force flows more strongly to the facial area, the voice is strengthened, the eyes and skin are brightened, and the mind tends to become clearer.

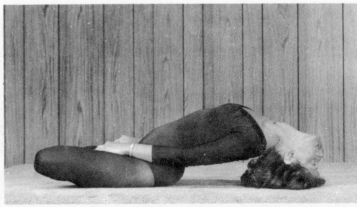

FORWARD BENDING (*PASCHIMOTTANASANA*)

Before beginning this posture, always make sure your legs and hip joints are sufficiently limber by practicing the Knee Stretch (*Bhadrasana*). While sitting on the floor, place the soles of your feet together, grasp your feet with your hands, pull your feet in as close to your body as possible, and bounce your legs gently to the floor. Keep your back very straight. Allow your thighs to stretch more fully with each bounce. Stop after several bounces and gently lower your forehead as close to your feet as possible (remember to visualize the completed pose and not to worry about your body response).

Remaining seated on the floor, with your right leg extended, bend your left leg, placing your foot on your right thigh. Gently bounce your left knee towards the floor several times. Repeat with your opposite leg. Do not strain but gently encourage your knees towards the floor. This exercise will give you a good idea as to just how flexible your knees, ankles, and hips are at the present moment, in addition to limbering the joints in these areas.

After these two warmups, you can sit with your legs stretched out in front of you for Forward Bending. Raise your arms up and somewhat behind your head, stretching your entire spine fully and gazing skyward. Bend forward, visualizing bending from your hip area (not from your waist) and placing the top half of your body flat on the bottom half. Keep your legs flat on the floor, even if you cannot bend as far forward then. Eventually your elbows will rest on the floor, your toes can be grasped and gently pulled towards your head, and your head and chest will rest on your legs. At first you may only be able to grasp your knees, calf muscles, or ankles. This is fine. Continue to visualize the completed pose and your body will soon approximate the pose. Above all, do not worry or hurry yourself too quickly. Consciously relax your leg muscles, back, and shoulder area. Send your breath to any areas of tightness. Remember not to force your body to bend too far at first; *flow* gently into the pose, hold it without strain, and *flow* easily out of it.

To complete Forward Bending, keep your head tucked towards your legs and, while bringing your arms up the outsides of your legs, uncurl your spine an inch at a time. Stretch your arms high up over your head again, feeling the stretch along the entire length of your spine, then slowly lower your arms back to your sides. Relax either lying on your back or by folding your legs, closing your eyes, and turning within. This pose can also be done from a standing position, in which case it is called Standing Forward Bending and is performed identically to Forward Bending from a sitting position. (See section on Miscellaneous Postures.)

Forward Bending massages all of the internal organs, tones the abdominal muscles, improves digestion, and helps aid in the correction of constipation and hemorrhoids. After the backwards bending of the Fish, *Paschimott-anasana* is an excellent counterpose and forward stretching posture for the spine. Again, it is the play of opposites to bring everything into evenness. Because of the tightness of the hamstring muscles in most people, this posture demonstrates the necessity of patience and the importance of self-acceptance. If held motionless for some length of time, a very calming effect upon the mind will be noted.

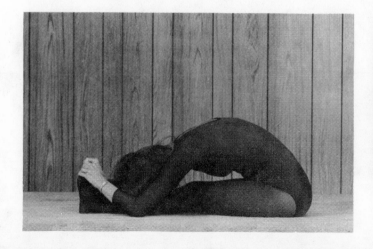

THE INCLINED PLANE (*KATIKASANA*)

Sit down comfortably with your arms on the floor directly under your shoulders. Gazing upwards, begin to raise your body up off the floor, weight on your arms and feet, until your body resembles an inclined plane. Try to flatten both your feet on the floor; your body will be supported by your hands and feet. Your head will be an extension of the straight line of your spine, and your body should not be allowed to sag at any point. Hold the pose without any undue strain. Lower your body gently back to the floor. Repeat once or twice more and rest in the Pose of a Child, this time extending your arms far out in front of your body. Be very aware of the life force circulating throughout your spine and into all of your extremities.

This pose affords an opposite stretch to the body after Forward Bending. It can help get rid of any kinks in the back, as well as strengthen the spine and wrists and firm the hips and abdomen.

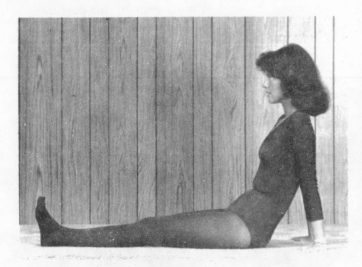 

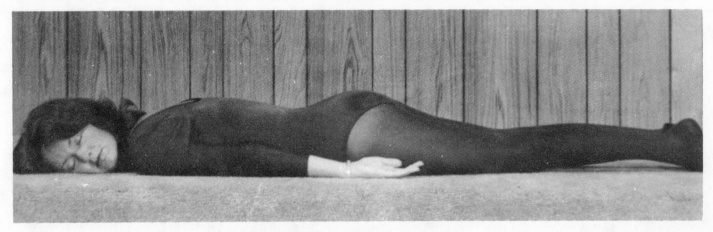

THE COBRA (*BHUJANGASANA*)

Lie relaxed on your stomach with your arms at your sides and your head turned comfortably either to your right or left side. Slide your feet and legs together easily, toes pointed, and lock your knees. Turn your head and touch your forehead to the floor, while your chin touches your chest and your hands are placed directly under your shoulders (your fingers should point towards each other if beginning and straight ahead if more advanced).

Put your attention on your upper back muscles and use them (instead of your hands) to arch your head and neck as far backwards as possible. Raise your chest up slowly, one vertebra at a time. Your elbows should remain close to your body, and your body, from the navel down, should remain on the floor. Curve the spine and stretch as far backwards as possible; look up at the ceiling (taking care again to relax your forehead muscles).

When ready to come back down, use your back muscles once more to lower your body slowly to the floor, an inch at a time. Bring your forehead back to touch the floor and your chin to touch your chest. Turn your head to the side and let your arms rest alongside your body. Breathe fully and completely. Allow your body to flow smoothly throughout the entire pose, with no resistance, straining, or forcing at any point.

Relax this time in *Savasana* while lying on your side. This is a variation of the Corpse Pose. If lying on your right side, extend your right arm up behind your head with your head resting easily on it. Your left arm should be placed comfortably behind your hip, on top of it, or on the floor in front of your body. (This is an ideal sleeping position since it removes stress from all parts of the body.) Close your eyes and turn completely within with total attention. Be aware of the increased flow of your vital-force, especially noticeable now in your upper back and shoulders.

A variation of the Cobra, once it can be executed and held for some time in its full position, is as follows: after your back is arched in the extreme position, allow your head to come forward and gaze straight ahead; rotate your head gently to the right and look as far over your shoulder as you are able; hold and rotate far to the left, looking over your left shoulder. Gently bring your head back to the center and lower your body, inch by inch and with eyes closed, stopping along the way to tune in with your body and really *feel* the life force in your spine. Complete the posture as before.

The Cobra, in its completed position, resembles a cobra snake about to strike. It reverses and completes the stretch just accomplished in Forward Bending. It increases the elasticity of the spine, especially concentrating on the upper back. It tones the abdominal muscles and encourages maximum function of the reproductive organs. It aids in reducing flatulence and helps align the spinal column correctly. It is also an excellent pose to follow the Shoulder Stand and to quickly and completely relax your body just before going to sleep, when you do not have time to complete a longer practice routine.

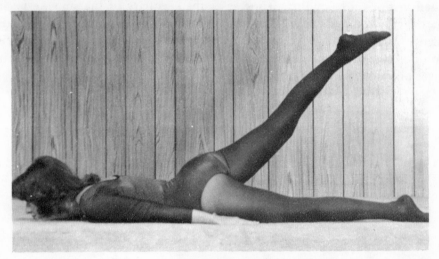

THE LOCUST (*SALABHASANA*)

Lie comfortably on your stomach. Place your chin on the floor, stretching it as far forward of your body as possible. Place your arms on the floor, palms down next to your thighs. Your legs should be extended together and your forehead relaxed. Transfer your attention to your lower back muscles, using only them to raise your right leg high up into the air. Your leg muscles should remain relaxed, and the pull should be felt in your lower back muscles. Extend your leg into the air starting from your hip area, making sure your abdomen, pelvis, chest, and chin remain on the floor. Hold comfortably; lower the leg and then raise your left leg in the same manner. Do this three times, alternating on the right and left sides of your body until you can hold the pose motionless for a longer time. This is the Half Locust.

The Full Locust is a more difficult pose and one of the few *Yogasanas* where a degree of effort and force are applied. Lie on your stomach as before, chin extended. Make fists with your hands, placing them under your thighs. Inhale, stiffen your body, and thrust both legs into the air without bending them. Your body weight is on your chest and arms. Retain this position for a few seconds, rest, and repeat. This pose may be practiced after proficiency is gained in the Half Locust and after you have gained greater body strength, but it is not a necessity. The Half Locust will be equally beneficial to your body.

The Locust follows the Cobra to complete the stretching of the lower back and is so named because of its resemblance to a locust when resting on the ground. While the Cobra and Locust both strengthen the spine and make it more flexible, the Locust concentrates on the lumbar region, while the Cobra concentrates on the upper back area. The abdominal muscles and the pelvis are toned, as are the hip and thigh areas. Weak lower backs are a common complaint of many people today. Daily practice of the Locust (or Half Locust) can help strengthen the lower back and alleviate the resulting nervous tension often concentrated there.

"How beautiful upon the mountains are the feet of him that bringeth good tidings."
        — *Isaiah III, 7*

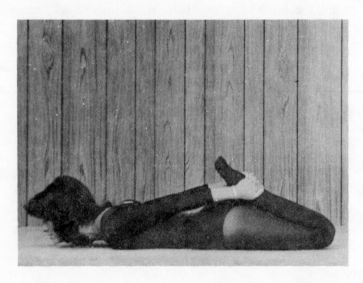

THE BOW (*DHANAURASANA*)

Lie on your stomach and be totally relaxed. Take a few complete breaths. Bend your legs and gently grasp your ankles with each hand. Your feet should remain together. Slowly raise your head, chest and thighs up off the floor, keeping your arms straight and letting your legs pull your body up and off the floor. (Visualize pulling the bowstring on a bow). Arch your back and allow all your body weight to rest on your abdomen, not on your chest, ribs, or thighs. Gaze skyward while keeping your forehead relaxed. Feel the stretch down the full length of your body.

Remain in the pose as long as comfortable; slowly and with control, lower your thighs back to the floor, followed by your chest, and finally by your chin. Release your legs and lower them gently back to the floor. Turn your head to one side and be aware of your entire spinal area and of the vital-force within your body. Relax totally and be the conscious silent witness to this moment.

 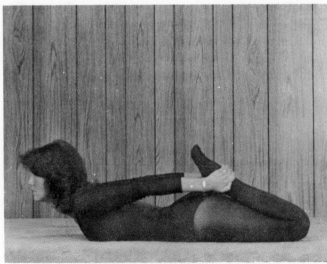

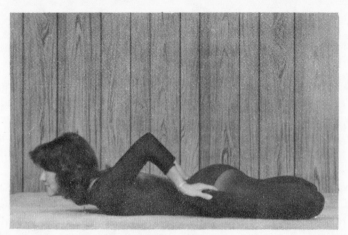

As a variation to complete the Bow: after your thighs, chest, and chin have been lowered to the floor, continue holding your ankles and attempt to press your feet *gently* down to the floor on either side of your hips. Be sure to wait until your body and ankles have become quite limber and accustomed to the bending in this pose, however.

Do not be in a hurry to execute the Bow perfectly. Take it gently, flowing in one continuous motion and allowing time for your body to adjust to the more extreme bending. Keep your mind off physical progress and stay in present time. Then you will realize real progress quickly and easily. After you have become adept at this pose, you can rock on your stomach very simply by breathing easily in and out; the rocking will occur naturally with the rhythm of breathing and need not be forced by straining the neck and head up and down.

The Bow is the third in the series of bending for the back. Dhana means bow, which is what the body resembles in the completed position of the posture. The Bow limbers and strengthens the entire spine at one time; thus the body receives all the benefits of the Cobra and Locust Pose and more: a certain inner resiliency. It also helps reduce abdominal fat and loosens the hip joints. Done in conjunction with the Cobra and the Locust, the Bow helps to correct menstrual disorders and the accompanying stress from the monthly cycle that sometimes troubles women.

THE HALF SPINAL TWIST (*ARDHA MATSYENDRASANA*)

Sit comfortably with both legs extended in front of your body. (Make sure your body rests evenly on both sides of your buttocks, otherwise the twist will not be complete.) Bend your right leg and place it on the outside of your left knee. Bring your left arm up over and in front of your right leg; then twist your arm gently, bringing it around the bent right leg and grasping your right ankle or the foot of your right leg.

Twist your trunk gently to the right, placing your right arm behind your back at the waist area and around as close to your left thigh as possible. Look up over your right shoulder, forehead muscles relaxed. Hold for a few moments and feel the twist in your entire spine; turn your head gently back to the front, followed by your arms and body, finally uncrossing and extending your legs. Think always of flowing in the posture, never straining or jerking. Send your breath to any resistance and allow your body to relax. Now bend and cross your left leg and twist in the opposite direction. Do this two or three times on each side of your body. This is the beginning Half Spinal Twist.

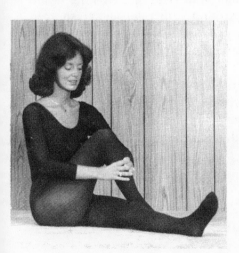 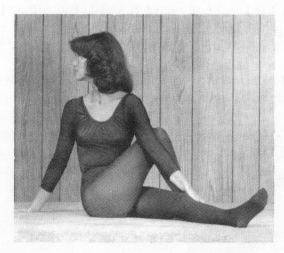 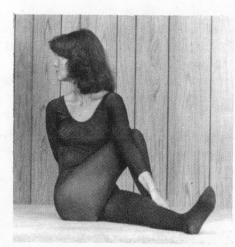

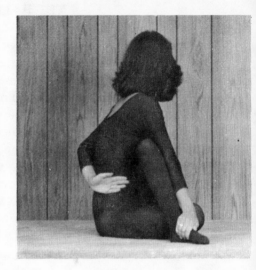

When your body has adjusted with some proficiency to the Half Twist, the pose may be practiced as follows: Begin as before, sitting squarely on your seat with your legs extended forward. Bend your left leg, placing it on the floor with the sole of your left foot against your body next to your groin. Bend your right leg, crossing it and placing it on the outside of your left knee; fold your left arm in front of and around your right leg; grasp your right calf, ankle, or foot; turn your head and body gently as far to the right as you are able without strain, your right arm again behind the waist, and look up and over your right shoulder. Flow smoothly back out of the pose and twist to the left.

Although this pose is difficult to describe easily in words, it can be followed easily in the photographs and is one of the most graceful *Yogasanas* when executed smoothly and calmly. The twisting affords a unique turn to the spine and body not found in any other postures. Abdominal muscles are toned; hip joints are lubricated and loosened; back muscles are strengthened; and the curing of constipation is aided. *Ardha Matsyendrasana* is named for a *yogi* who was called *Matsyendra.*

CONCLUDING THE PRACTICE LESSON

The Spinal Twist is the last pose in the regular order of this practice lesson. When time allows, a few miscellaneous poses may be added at this point. These exercises can then be followed by the practice of *pranayama* and, finally, by relaxation and/or meditation.

Included in the following sections are Sitting Postures, additional poses which may be substituted or added to the regular order of practice (the Pelvic Stretch, for instance, a backward stretch, may be substituted for the Fish), Balancing Postures, Facial Exercises, techniques for *Pranayama*, relaxation, and meditation.

The lesson just outlined is intended to serve as an example for you to follow. You may vary the poses for the sake of variety as long as you retain the basic order: inverse posture (or postures); backward bending; forward bending; Cobra, Locust and Bow; twisting postures (or posture); relaxation whenever necessary during practice; miscellaneous postures when time allows; concluding with *pranayama*, relaxation, and meditation.

"Ask, and ye shall receive, that your joy may be full."

— John XI, 24

SITTING POSTURES (MEDITATIVE POSES)

The following section contains Sitting Postures, sometimes called Meditative Poses because many of them can be used when one sits quietly to meditate. The process of meditation will be explained at the conclusion of this book, but, for the purpose of easier explanation of some of the poses to follow this section, the Sitting Postures are examined and explained now.

EASY POSTURE (*SUKHASANA*)

Sit in a relaxed position on your buttocks with your legs stretched forward. Bend your legs and cross them comfortably, knees resting on your insteps. Keep your back straight (but not rigid or stiff) and your head in a straight line with your spine. Sit quietly, being aware of all the internal processes occurring within your system.

This is the most basic as well as the easiest Sitting or Meditation Pose. Meditation is the process of turning within to the real source of one's being, becoming still and having insight into the nature of *all* that is. In the East, young people grow up sitting regularly in this cross-legged position. In the West, most people are unaccustomed to sitting on the floor and may find it hard to do so at first, especially for long periods of time. Easy Posture will support the body (keeping it firm and straight) equally as well as some of the more difficult Sitting Poses. Since one purpose of *Hatha Yoga* is to prepare the body to sit motionless in meditation, many find this simple Sitting Posture to be most useful. But any of the poses on the following pages that feel comfortable and natural may be used.

In spare moments, while relaxing (perhaps watching television or sitting on the floor visiting with friends), try sitting in one of the postures in this section. They will hold your body firm without tiring it and can be useful aids in staying self-contained and in your own space no matter what is transpiring around you.

PERFECT POSTURE (*SIDDHASANA*)

Sit comfortably with your legs stretched forwards from your body; bend both legs inward towards your crotch. Let the heel of one foot rest on the top of the other and the soles of your feet turn upwards. Your legs should fit comfortably on top of each other and be in towards your crotch. Your head, neck, and body should be in a straight line. Your hands can either be folded in front of your body resting on your feet and legs, or you can rest with your arms stretched out on your knees, your thumb and forefinger locked in the Chin Mudra.

This pose, often called the Adepts' Pose, can be useful for long term sitting (as in meditation). It has been a favorite of saints and sages throughout the ages for meditation because it is easier to practice than some of the other meditative postures, yet it will keep the body in an upright and stable position. It will also beneficially stretch the muscles of the back and the legs, helping the body to relax.

THE FAVORABLE POSE (ANKLE LOCK) (*SWASTIKASANA*)

Sit with your legs outstretched. Bend your right leg and place the heel of your foot to the left of your groin, with the sole against your left thigh. Bend your left leg, place it over your right ankle, and let your left foot touch your right leg. Your left sole should rest between the calf and thigh; insert your leg gently between the calf and thigh. The toe of your right foot should be visible between your left calf and thigh. Your feet should rest comfortably against your inner thighs. Keep your spine and head in a straight line. Let your hands rest on your knees, in the closed finger position known as the Chin Mudra, or simply fold them in front of your body. You can also do this pose by bending your left leg first and crossing the right over it, proceeding as before.

Swastikasana is a good preparation for the Lotus Posture. Its literal meaning is favorable pose, so-called because the ankles cross each other at right angles, considered auspicious angles for favorable conditions. This is a useful pose for meditation if you find the Lotus too strenuous on your legs and ankles or if you have long limbs.

THE HALF LOTUS AND THE LOTUS POSE (*PADMASANA*)

From a comfortable seated position, bend your right leg, placing it in against your groin. Now bend your left leg, placing it up over and on your right thigh, close to the hip joint there. Bring your left foot as high up and as close to the trunk of your body as possible. Keep your bent left knee pointed downwards towards the floor as much as you are able. Place your hands on your knees in Chin Mudra, close your eyes, turn within, and relax. This is the Half Lotus Posture. You can reverse the posture by bending your left leg and crossing the right leg over it. Most people will have a natural preference to practice on one side or the other.

The Full Lotus should only be attempted when your hip, knee, and ankle joints have become fully limber. In the seated position, extend your right leg and cross your left leg up and over it as you did in Half Lotus. Gently grasp your right foot, bend your right leg, and cross it up over and on top of the left leg. Again, bring it as high and as close to the trunk of your body as possible. Both knees should remain on the floor eventually (though this may not be physically possible at first), and the soles of the feet should turn upwards. Your spine and neck should be in a straight line, and the palms of your hands can be placed on your knees: thumb and forefinger locked on the knees with the other three fingers extended in the Chin Mudra; or your hands may be simply folded in front of your body and rested on your legs and feet.

Be certain that your hip joints, knees, ankles and feet are sufficiently limber before attempting this full pose, or it may cause too much stress on the joints in these areas. Placing a few small cushions under your buttocks may be useful to help elevate your body, so that your knees can remain on the floor with less stress in the lower part of your body. (You may have discovered that one knee rises off the floor or that both knees cannot be brought comfortably to the floor when seated flat on the floor.) Continued practice without anxiety for results will help your body to assume this pose more easily and completely.

The Lotus Pose is considered a perfect meditation pose, as well as a useful one in which to practice *pranayamas*. It locks the body into position, keeping it steady and preventing it from tiring and slumping forward when long periods of time are spent in deep meditation. The Lotus also aids digestion and improves the appetite, increases the flow of blood to the pelvis, and strengthens the muscles and nerves of the legs. The full pose is a rather strenuous pose and should be approached gently and with much patience and common sense.

THE KNEELING POSTURE (*VAJRASANA*)

Keeping your spine and head straight ahead, kneel on your ankles, forming a saddle for your seat. Your ankles should roll outwards with your feet relaxed and the big toes on each foot touching. Your knees should be together, with your arms resting comfortably on your knees. Sit down easily and gently upon your legs. If your ankles are stiff, practice conditioning exercises for them, such as ankle rolls and the skiing exercise. Proceed slowly; know your body's flexibility and do not force your body to remain very long in this posture until your legs and feet have become quite limber.

You may find this to be a very comfortable sitting pose. It aids in keeping the ankles and feet flexible and strong and the muscles in the legs and thighs firm. Since the ankles are one of the first parts of the body to show signs of aging. *Vajrasana* can help retard the psychological aging process. It also helps reduce flatulence, aids in digestion, and helps to condition the entire nervous system.

Whenever ironing, try kneeling in this posture, placing the ironing board almost on the floor and working from this height and position. Notice how much less tiring this is on the body than is standing up. It also helps to prevent low back strain which can result from standing unbalanced with the hip cocked to one side.

THE HEROIC POSE (VEERASANA)

Sit comfortably on the floor. Bend your left leg, folding it back so that your left heel rests against your right leg and buttock. Cross your right leg over your left, letting the top of your right foot rest on the floor. Interlock your fingers and grasp your knees. Keep your spine and neck in a straight line, firm but relaxed.

This pose is said to give control over the sexual urge, as well as greatly benefit the gonads (sex glands). It can also be a very comfortable pose in which just to sit as soon as the body adjusts to it.

THE FROG POSE (*MANDUKASANA*)

Kneel on the floor. Sit with your knees spread widely apart. The tops of your feet should be on the floor, and your toes should meet behind your back. Place your hands on your knees and sit comfortably on your buttocks. Remember to send your breath to any part of your body that feels tight, consciously relaxing it.

The Frog Pose will help flex and strengthen the hip, knee, and ankle joints. It will also aid in strengthening the lower back area. One should give the body time to adjust to this sitting position, not sitting long enough initially to result in any pain (there may be some awareness of stiffness in the ankles until they loosen sufficiently). The tightness in the lower body generally takes some time to loosen, and one should always exercise extreme patience and gentleness here.

ADDITIONAL AND MISCELLANEOUS POSTURES FOR PRACTICE

INVERSE POSTURE: THE UNSUPPORTED SHOULDER STAND (*NIRALAMBA SARVANGASANA*)

Begin lying relaxed on your back as you did in the Shoulder Stand. Slowly raise your legs into the air over your head, straightening your back and pressing your chin tightly into your chest. Gaze at your toes. When you are comfortable and balanced in this position, slowly begin to raise your arms up off the floor, taking care to maintain your balance on your shoulders, neck, and head; place the palms of your hands on top of your thighs. You may need to tilt your torso slightly backwards to adjust for balance. Hold this posture (again, never to the point of strain); lower your arms carefully back to the floor; bring your knees to your forehead, keep your head and neck on the floor; and begin to unwind your spine an inch at a time as you did in the Shoulder Stand, placing your body gently and fully back on the floor again.

Niralamba Sarvangasana is an *asana* for more advanced practitioners. You should not attempt it until you can remain motionless in the full Shoulder Stand for quite some time, and your back, neck and shoulders have become very strong. Benefits to the body and internal systems will be the same for both postures, but the Unsupported Shoulder Stand puts additional pressure on the neck and entire shoulder area, cleansing, revitalizing, and encouraging the more complete flow of vital-force within these areas. Tune into your body, know its limits at the moment, and take care not to force your body too quickly into this *asana*.

BACKWARD BENDING: THE PELVIC STRETCH (*SUPTA VAJRASANA*)

With your feet together, kneel on your feet and legs in Kneeling Posture, hands resting on your knees. Place your hands on the floor on either side of your feet; gently arch your body upwards, pressing into your arms and legs and bringing your pelvis up off the floor. Gaze skyward, with your forehead relaxed, and keep your arms straight to help support your weight. Hold this position as long as comfortable without strain; return to Kneeling Posture and rest in Pose of a Child, head to the side and arms alongside your body.

When this position can be held easily, you can begin by sitting in Kneeling Posture, spreading your legs and sitting on the floor between your feet, gently coming back onto your elbows, and allowing your head to hang back. Again, raise the trunk of the body up off the floor and stretch. Hold this position only as long as it is comfortable; stretch forward and rest sufficiently.

The most extreme pelvic stretch is accomplished by sitting between your feet and gently stretching all the way back until your shoulders and head touch the floor. Try to keep your knees together and lock your arms over your head, thereby arching your back upwards and bringing your head closer to your feet.

Pelvic stretches are excellent postures for removing tension and stress from the body. They increase the flexibility of the hips, legs and feet, and firm the muscles of the hips and thighs. They also tone the internal organs and beneficially affect the glands and nerves. Any one or all of these stretches can be substituted in the regular order of practice for backward bending (the Fish was done in our practice lesson).

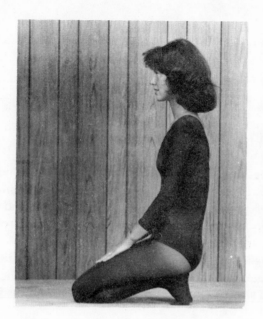

BACKWARD BENDING: THE RABBIT POSE (*SASANGASANA*)

Begin in Keeling Posture. Rise up onto your knees and curl your toes under. Slowly and with steady control, bend your body backwards, all the while gazing up towards the ceiling. Grasp the left ankle with your left hand and the right ankle with your right hand. Arch your body upwards and feel the flow of vital-force circulating throughout your system; stretch. Hold for a few moments; gently release your ankles; lower your body back to a kneeling position, all the while with total control; stretch forward in Pose of a Child to bend your body in the opposite direction and allow it to relax totally. Close your eyes and observe any changes this posture has made within your body.

Sasangasana will increase flexibility of the spine, strengthen the back, legs and feet, and tone the abdominal muscles. It will also encourage complete breathing by forcing the lungs to expand to their full capacity and get rid of any stale air (excess carbon dioxide) left behind by shallow and incomplete breathing.

The Rabbit Pose may be substituted for other backward bending poses in the regular order of practice or used as an additional one.

FORWARD BENDING: THE GREAT SEAL (*MODIFIED MAHA MUDRA*)

Sit on the floor with your legs outstretched. Bend your left leg and place the heel at the juncture between the genitals and the anus. Stretch your arms high up over your head (as in Forward Bending) and lean forward, grasping your toes if at all possible. Remember to think of bending from your hip area and flattening the top of your body onto your legs. This makes bending much easier than bending from the waist. Keep your legs on the floor. Relax and hold as long as comfortable; uncurl your spine an inch at a time, bringing your arms up the outsides of your legs; straighten your left leg, bend your right, and repeat the pose on the opposite side of your body; finally, extend both legs and bend forward to complete the pose.

Modified Maha Mudra will encourage the life force to flow upwards in the body. It will aid in problems of constipation, hemorrhoids, indigestion, and other abdominal difficulties. It can be performed in addition to or in place of the other forward bending *asanas*.

"Possess your soul with patience."
— John Dryden

FORWARD BENDING: THE HEAD TO KNEE POSE (*JANU SIRASANA*)

Sit on the floor with your legs stretched forward. Bend your left leg, placing your heel on the floor against the groin and the sole against the side of your right thigh. (As you become more limber, you can place the foot on top of the thigh.) Stretch your arms high above your head, again stretching your entire spine as in forward bending with *Paschimottasana*. Bend forward, always visualizing bending from your hip area, and lower your forehead to your knee (or as close as it will comfortably come), grasping your right toe with your fingers. Relax. Do not strain; flow with the mental image of water, which moves with no resistance. Keep your right leg on the floor. The stretch is more beneficial if you keep your extended leg flat on the floor, even if you cannot bend so far at first as you would like. Give yourself time and your body will respond more completely. Send your breath to any areas of resistance. Hold this pose as long as it is comfortable for you; repeat, extending your left leg this time and bending your right. Rest in the Corpse Pose, turning completely within for a sufficient amount of time.

Perhaps you will notice that it is easier for your body to bend either to your right or left side; this is normal for most people. Alternate Forward Bending can help you spot any tight areas in your body which might benefit from a little added concentration. After stretching two or three times in each direction, rest. Be patient with this *asana* and yourself, and practice until you can hold it easily in both directions for at least thirty seconds to a minute.

Janu Sirasana will stimulate the internal organs and encourage correct function of the liver, pancreas, and kidneys. It will also stretch the body muscles and aid in the relief of constipation. It can be used as an alternate pose to simple Forward Bending.

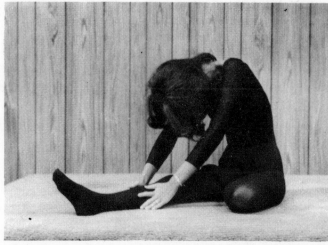

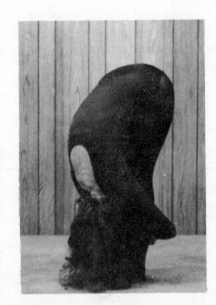

STANDING FORWARD BENDING: *(PADAHASTHASANA)*

Stand erect with your feet together. Slowly raise your arms high up and back over your head (stretching the full length of your spine) and lean slightly backwards. Visualize your spine being stretched out to its entire length.

Lean forward slowly, leading with your head, and, keeping your legs straight, attempt to press your head gently to your knees and grasp your toes. Visualize bending from your hip area, so that your entire upper body folds down easily upon your legs. Consciously relax your entire body. You can clasp your hands behind your legs and gently bounce your body down toward your legs if you have any difficulty bending very far forward at first. Do not bend your legs; if you do, the stretch will not be a full one and some of the benefits of the pose may be lost. Breathe naturally while retaining this pose for a few moments. Tell your legs to relax. Tell your shoulders and entire back to relax and send your breath to any points of resistance. Stand up slowly, keeping your head tucked and letting your arms come up the outsides of your legs. Uncurl your spine an inch at a time. Stand very still, close your eyes, and observe the changes this pose has made on the flow of life force in your body. Practice this posture until you are able to hold it for a longer time without strain. Give your body time to adjust to it, without being impatient for results.

Padahasthasana is Forward Bending from a standing position, and, perhaps as you were then, you may be aware of tight hamstring muscles in your legs. Do not worry about them. Practice slowly and gently, without allowing any negative thoughts to enter your mind. Be patient, stay in present time awareness, and your body will soon conform to the completed pose. The body receives all the regular benefits of Forward Bending with Standing Forward Bending, in addition to an increase in the flow of blood and vital-force to the upper body and head. This will benefit all the body organs, rest the heart, and help to calm and clear the mind. *Padahasthasana* will also generally tone the entire body.

TWISTING: THE TRIANGULAR POSTURE (*TRIKONASANA*)

Stand with your feet spread widely apart. Slowly raise your arms (left palm up and right palm down) to shoulder level, gazing straight ahead.

Raise your left arm high above your head and, looking at your left palm, bend your body to the right, letting your right hand slide down your right leg until it reaches your foot (or as far down the leg as you are able to stretch without strain). Your arm should be directly over your left ear and parallel to the floor. Continue to watch your left palm; hold; feel the stretch; raise your body slowly and with control upright again, bringing your arms back to shoulder level; lower them; remain still and relax for a moment, being totally conscious and aware in the moment.

Repeat the posture on your left side this time, with your right arm raised and your body bending to the left. Do this two or three more times on either side of your body, always being aware of your own immediate physical limits and observing quietly any increased awareness in the harmony of your internal systems. Stand, close your eyes, and rest quietly (remember to focus your eyes internally so as not be become dizzy).

You can vary this posture by twisting your torso. Begin as in *Trikonasana*, bringing your arms to shoulder level with wrists flexed upwards. Twist the trunk of your body as far as possible to the right. Place your left hand on the floor beside your right foot, your right arm extended vertically and next to your ear. Gaze easily skyward over your right arm. (Get inside your body and *feel* this stretch in your spine.) Hold as long as comfortable; straighten your torso, again with arms at shoulder level; lower your arms; close your eyes and relax. Twist identically to your left and then stand quietly, being aware of all the vitality circulating within and throughout your system.

Trikonasana is another twisting pose that, in addition to the Half Spinal Twist, affords great benefit to the abdominal muscles and organs. It increases peristalsic action of the bowels, improves the appetite, and increases the sideways flexibility of the spine.

*"The past is memory, the
future is yet to be experienced,
today only is real to us."*
                    — Roy Eugene Davis

THE COW HEAD POSE (*GOMUKHASANA*)

Sit in Kneeling Position or the Heroic Pose. Slowly and deliberately raise your arms out in front of your body to shoulder level; bring the left one back behind your back and place it just above the waist (palm outward); lift the right one upward, allowing it to fold down from your shoulder, palm against your back; attempt to clasp the fingers of both hands at a comfortable point. In the completed position, your forearms should be brought as parallel to your spine as possible. Relax your entire body. Hold the pose only as long as it is comfortable for you, release your hands gently, and bring your arms back to rest on your knees. Gently massage any tight areas of which you are aware. Relax a moment and reverse the pose, lifting your left arm upwards this time and folding your right arm behind your waist. Always remember to relax into the pose.

For an extra pull on your shoulders, arms, and back, after you have become proficient in this pose, lean forward and attempt to place your elbow on the floor above your head, while still clasping the fingers and kneeling. Hold this stretch only as long as comfortable, sit up and repeat, leading with the opposite elbow.

This pose will loosen all the muscles and joints in the shoulder area, keeping it supple and strong. Most people will notice that it is easier to perform this posture reaching up first with either the right or left arm, since one side of the body is often looser than the other. It is useful to become aware of all the body parts during practice. Use the *asanas* to spot any tight areas and tension occurring with them. Consciously relax these areas. Continue practicing without being anxious for results, and both sides of the body will eventually come into evenness, and stress and resulting tension in the back and neck area will slip away.

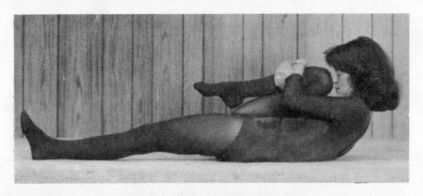
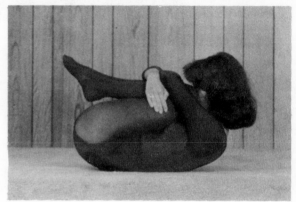
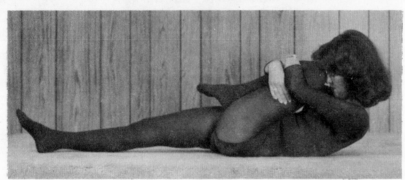

THE WIND RELIEVING POSE (*VATAYNASANA*)

Lie flat on your back and relax completely. Inhale deeply and bend your right leg, raising it up and placing it as close to your chest and abdomen as possible. Retain your breath and grasp your right leg, pressing it tightly into your chest and abdomen. Raise your head up gently from the floor and try to touch your forehead to your knee. Your left leg should remain flat on the floor throughout this procedure. Hold for a few moments and exhale, releasing your right leg and slowly extending it, lowering it gently back to the floor.

Repeat this posture, bending your left leg this time and touching it to your forehead; complete the pose by bending and holding both your legs, curling onto your spine as though it were a ball, and touching both knees to your forehead (or as close as you are able to come).

Repeat each of these procedures two to three times and rest, eyes closed, in *Savasana*, all the while being aware of the energy which forms your body and is circulating within.

The Wind Relieving Pose will strengthen the muscles and organs in the abdomen. It will also aid in relieving gas or flatulence in the stomach and lower abdomen and improve evacuation.

THE STOMACH LIFT (*UDDIYANA BANDHA*)

Stand with your feet a foot or two apart. Bend your legs slightly and lean forward, placing your hands on top of your thighs. Illustrated here is an alternate way to practice in a seated posture. Concentrate and exhale completely, emptying the air *entirely* from your lungs (feel as though your chest cavity is hollow). A tightness or constriction can be felt in your neck and upper chest area when the air is properly expelled from your chest. Pull your abdominal cavity in as far as it will go and then lift it up, as though to place it inside the chest cavity against your backbone. Do not inhale while pulling in the abdomen. You will not be able to pull it in correctly unless the lungs are completely emptied. Your abdomen should look like the inside of a spoon; visualize it touching your backbone and being up inside your chest cavity. Remember to pull in *only* your abdominal area. Your lower intestinal area and the rest of your body should remain relaxed. Think of two movements: back and up. Retain this position for a few seconds, relax your abdomen, and empty the lungs again. Do this several times until you can flow into the position and hold it easily. Do not retain the position too long at first. Hold only a moderate amount of time. You will be able to retain your breath longer as you build your general body endurance.

Practice the next stage by repeating several rapid in and out movements of the abdominal area with each retention of breath. Do only about ten contractions at first. Later you may be able to do forty, fifty, or even more on a single retention, but do not be in a hurry at first. Let this happen naturally as you progress.

The Stomach Lift will energize your body, giving you much available energy and more in reserve. It will help increase the powers of digestion and will beneficially massage the internal abdominal area. It will aid in reducing the waistline. Make sure to practice this *asana* on an empty stomach. Done first thing in the morning upon arising (after drinking a glass of warm water to which a little lemon juice has been added), the Stomach Lift will encourage peristaltic action and natural, regular elimination.

INVERSE POSTURE: THE HEADSTAND (*SIRSASANA*)

This is a pose for advanced practitioners only. When you first attempt to perform the Headstand, you would do well to practice against a wall. The idea is not to become dependent upon the wall, but to allow yourself a safe place to practice until all the muscles of your body (especially the neck, shoulders and arms) have become accustomed to this pose. If you are certain that you already have the necessary balance and coordination for this posture, you should still practice in an area clear of furniture or any other objects which might result in injury should you momentarily lose your balance.

Practice each stage of the Headstand for several days, giving your body time to get used to the pose gradually and time to develop the necessary coordination and strength to perform this *asana* correctly.

Kneel with your toes curled under and interlace your fingers. Place your hands on the floor in front of your body, forming an equilateral triangle with your arms (this three point position will be steadier for most people than balancing on the hands and head alone). Place the crown of your head firmly on the floor with your fingers and hands cupping the back of your head (experiment a little to find the most comfortable and even placement).

Straighten your legs and walk forward gently, until the trunk of your body becomes nearly vertical; then continue to walk until you feel as though your body may tip over backwards (of course, you should not: stop before reaching this point). Remain in this position for a moment, bend your legs back to the kneeling position, lower your body gently, and rest in the Pose of a Child, head turned to the side. Practice in this manner for several days until your body has time to feel natural and at ease in the upside down position. Holding this simple position will strengthen your shoulders and neck, giving you a better sense of balance and necessary confidence to continue with the pose.

Never be in a hurry with the Headstand; proceed slowly, knowing your current limits, and allow your body time to become strong enough to perform the entire *asana* with poise and complete self-control and without toppling out of it at any point.

After your body becomes accustomed to the inverted position and you have walked back to the point where your trunk is vertical and slightly backwards, lift your feet slowly up off the floor, bend your knees, and carefully fold them next to your chest. This will take a certain amount of strength. Practice holding this position as long as you can for several days in a row; make sure you can remain in this position with perfect control for a minute or longer before going any further. This will insure that your neck and shoulders become strong enough and that you can balance more naturally when you are fully upside down.

When you have become entirely comfortable in the preceding position, slowly raise your legs until they are in a horizontal position over your body with the knees still bent. Remain motionless at this point for as long as you are able, repeating the pose to this point several days in a row; be able to remain steady easily for a minute or so without any wobbling. Watch your breathing and stay entirely self-contained.

 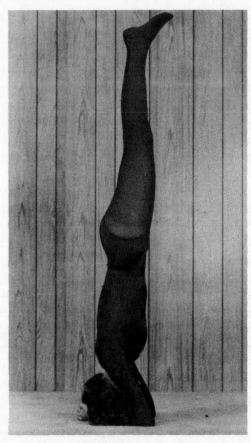

The final movement is to straighten your legs very slowly up over your head, maintaining balance, until your entire body is stretched out upside down. Never jerk your legs up suddenly. Stay in tune with your body, breathe normally, and focus your attention on one point, either with your eyes open or closed. Remain in this position for only a few moments in the beginning. Do not allow your body to bend or to sway at all while in this inverse position.

To complete the Headstand, bend your knees above your body and begin to come out of the posture slowly and with total self-control. Flow out of the pose in reverse order: lower your legs and bring your knees back to your chest. Remain for a moment in this position. Come down calmly, with total self-containment and total control of your body at all times. There will be added pressure on your arms and elbows as you lower your feet back to the floor from your chest. Do not give in to any tendency of your body to tumble down at this point.

Lower your feet and legs back to the floor, turn your toes under, assume a kneeling position, turn your head to one side, and rest completely in Pose of a Child (for up to a full minute or more). Never get up suddenly from the Headstand, since the sudden rush of blood and vital-force down from your head area can result in dizziness or even fainting. Practice each stage faithfully and completely, until you can flow through the entire posture gracefully and smoothly, and give yourself plenty of time to do so.

The Headstand is often called the *King* of the *Asanas*. Like the Shoulder Stand, it has an invigorating effect upon the entire system. It reverses the usual downward flow of gravity and tones the entire nervous system. It has a beneficial effect upon the endocrine glands and helps promote healthy brain tissue. Pressure on all the internal organs is relieved, and many diseases of the body are improved and relieved.

You may discover it useful to practice the Headstand after the regular *asanas*, holding it as long as you are comfortably able. But it does take much strength and coordination. Do not practice this posture if you ever have a headache or fever is present in your body, if overweight, or if troubled with cataracts or problems in your neck. If you are bothered by any of the preceding, you can receive equal benefits from the Shoulder Stand (or, if even this position is not possible, from lying on a slant board ten to twenty minutes a day). *Sirsasana* is an advanced pose listed for those who wish to try it, are physically qualified to do so, and able to follow their common sense at all times.

YOGA MUDRA (*THE YOGIC SEAL*)

Sit first in any comfortable cross-legged position (Easy Posture, Lotus. Half Lotus, or Perfect Posture). Gently bring your arms behind your body, holding your left wrist with your right hand. Slowly and gracefuly bend forward, lowering your chest towards the floor. Touch your forehead to the floor, if possible, then your chin. It does not matter how far you can bend; visualize the completed pose; relax and allow gentle practice to bring results. Hold the pose for a comfortable length of time; sit up slowly, close your eyes, and notice any changes in the flow of life force in your body.

Yoga Mudra can be practiced after the Headstand as a counterpose. It will aid in curing problems of constipation and will tone the entire nervous system. It will also aid in overcoming many disorders of the internal organs of the body. Follow Yoga Mudra with *Savasana*.

Any of these can be added at the end of your regular practice, if you have time or feel so inclined.

THE EAGLE POSE (*GARUDASANA*)

Fix your gaze on a point in front of your body. Standing with your spine stretched fully upward, bend your right leg slightly at the knee and place your entire body weight on this leg. Slowly and carefully wrap your left leg around in front of your right, continue on behind your leg, and rest your left foot on the calf muscles of your right supportive leg. Place your left arm up near your face with the palm facing towards the right and the thumb near your ear. After bringing your right arm under your left elbow, entwine both arms until the palms almost touch. Hold this position steadily for a few moments, slowly release your arms and legs, and come back to a standing position, always being careful to maintain your balance. Do not forget to keep your attention fixed on a point in front of your body and never remain in the pose so long that you lose your self-control and tumble out of it. Let your body become stronger gradually. Close your eyes, turn inside, rest a few moments, and repeat the pose, this time putting all your weight on your left leg.

The Eage Pose will strengthen your legs and thighs. It will increase coordination and give you better balance, poise, and self-control.

Always remember to relax completely into this and every posture you practice.

130

THE TREE POSE (*VRIKSASANA*)

Stand in a relaxed position with your spine erect. Fix your attention on a point, either a few feet in front of you on the floor or straight ahead at eye level on the wall. This focuses your attention and helps keep your body steady. Pick up your left foot and place it firmly on your right thigh just above your knee.

After your body is balanced, grasp your left foot and place it high up on your right thigh near your hip joint. Your foot should be turned so that the sole faces upwards. Slowly straighten your back, lowering your bent knee down as close to your right knee as you are able. Raise your arms up gracefully over your head, palms together. Stretch your entire spine upwards fully. Hold for a few moments, lower your arms, straighten your left leg, and place it gently back on the floor. Repeat the process, this time bending your right leg and placing it on your left leg. Come out of the pose gracefully and totally self-contained. Do not allow your body to collapse in an ungainly fashion. Keeping your attention one-pointed will make it easy to do. Pause, after completing the pose at least twice on both sides of your body, and observe further changes within the body.

The Tree Pose requires a certain amount of flexibility in the joints of the hips, ankles, and knees. It tones and strengthens all of the leg muscles, and it will improve your general sense of balance. One of the main reasons for practicing balancing is to improve general concentration and to gain better control of the body: to be able to bring all of your attention in to a single point and to remain motionless at that point. In Sanskrit, *Vriksa* means tree, so *Vriksasana* means to hold as motionless as a tree. You can think of the degree of steadiness with which you perform any balancing posture as a good indication of just how together you are at the present moment. When your mind is active, your body cannot be still. Balancing postures can help you become centered, focus your attention, quiet your body and mind, and enable you to remain motionless with poise and self-control.

THE DANCER POSE (*NATARAJASANA*)

Stand erect with your spine stretched out fully. Raise your right foot back and up off the floor, reach back with your right hand, and grasp your right foot. Focus your attention on a point directly in front of you in order to maintain your balance.

Holding your right foot firmly, begin to pull your entire right leg up towards the ceiling and out away from your buttocks. Gently raise your left arm high into the air, stretching your entire spine fully; stand tall and do not bend forward at all. Maintain this position for a few moments, remaining calm and steady. Slowly lower your right arm and leg, placing your foot back on the floor; stand still, close your eyes, and observe any changes this pose has made on different parts of your body. Repeat the process, this time lifting and stretching your left foot upward.

The Dancer Pose, like the Tree Pose, requires a considerable degree of flexibility in the hips and legs, plus a strong back. Proceed easily in the practice of this posture, never forcing or straining any part of your body. One movement that may be more noticeable than usual is the slight stretching of the knees and thighs, but there should be no pain at any point. The Dancer Pose will help strengthen the back, hips, and legs. It will help open the nasal passages, encouraging them to drain if necessary. It will also aid in the circulation of vital-force from the feet to the head, encouraging life force to flow more strongly upwards into the head, clearing and refreshing the mind.

ANGLE BALANCE (*VARIATION OF PASCHIMOTTANASANA*)

Sit squarely on your buttocks. Fix your attention firmly on a point in front of your eyes. Bend your knees, bringing them towards your chest and grasping your ankles or toes.

Maintaining perfect balance on your buttocks, carefully lift your legs up off the floor into the air and stretch them out slowly and fully while still holding your ankles or toes. Feel the stretch all down your spine and into your legs and feet.

After your legs have been fully straightened, slowly attempt to bring your knees to your forehead. Do not be in a hurry or let your attention wander. Your body should never topple unnaturally to the floor. Proceed steadily. Hold for a few moments and breathe naturally. To come out of the pose: bend your legs slowly and lower them back to the floor; release your ankles or toes; relax, observing further changes in your body due to this posture.

In the completed position, your arms may also be folded acrosss your chest, while your legs are extended together in the air and balance is maintained in this manner.

Angle Balancing will help develop good powers of mental concentration. It will also strengthen the legs, stomach, arms, and back. Vital-force will flow upward, aiding in overcoming impotency and helping to convert strong sexual energy into more subtle life force.

THE PEACOCK POSE (*MAYURASANA*)

Kneel and place your palms flat on the floor. Let your fingers point backwards and have your elbows together, placed between your knees. Rock your body gently and slowly forward until your forehead touches the floor. Your upper arms will support your chest and your elbows will press into your stomach.

Extend your legs backwards with your toes on the floor and let them rise up off and parallel to the floor, simultaneously raising your head up and looking forward. The forearms will now support your entire body. Hold without undue strain; slowly lower your legs, head, entire body; relax completely in *Savasana*, turning all your awareness within.

The Peacock Pose is a somewhat difficult pose, and care and restraint should be exercised whenever performing it. It is an advanced pose, and you should be quite flexible and strong before even attempting it. It is not a pose advised for most women because of the extra stress placed on the abdomen and pelvic organs. Those of you who do practice this pose will find it an excellent way to tone the entire body at once, especially the adominal area.

THE CROW (*KAKASANA*)

Squat on the floor on your toes. Place your arms about a shoulder's width apart, with your fingers spread and pointing forward to balance your body. Your knees may protrude slightly outside your elbows. Look forward, bringing your head up and fixing the gaze on a point in front of your body.

Gently rock forward and let your knees rest on your upper arms. Let your feet come up off the floor, with your entire body weight now resting on your hands and arms. Your toes may either touch or not. Keep your head up and your attention fixed throughout the entire *asana*. (You may need to do some experimentation to find the correct placement of your knees on your upper arms to allow you to rock forward and balance evenly.) Your lower arms remain straight, wrists firm, and your upper arms are slightly bent, so that they are able to bear the weight of your knees comfortably and your knees will not slide off them. Balance only as long as comfortable; lower your feet back to the floor, relax your entire body in one of the relaxation *asanas*, and observe further changes in your body. Be totally conscious of the moment. Practice steadily until coordination improves. Do this posture slowly, with poise and perfect control.

The Crow will develop strong wrists and arms, as well as greatly improve general body coordination. Since it does not require great strength (but more balance and coordination), it is fairly simple to execute when you locate the correct placement of your knees and arms. It will strengthen the shoulders and neck and is good preparation for the Headstand, strengthening the neck without direct pressure and demonstrating the type of balance that will be required should you proceed with the Headstand.

Beginners should take care in the practice of this posture not to rock too far forward and collapse onto the floor. If you feel that you lack necessary initial coordination, a pillow may be placed under your face until you have gained the balance and confidence to continue without it.

FACIAL EXERCISES

Any or all of the following may be chosen at the end of regular practice.

EYE EXERCISES

Sit in a comfortable position (perhaps Kneeling Posture or Easy Posture); allow your body to relax and your mind to become still. Place all of your attention in the area of your eyes. Proceed slowly and without strain of any kind. Keep your head still, allowing only your eyes to move in these exercises. Do each of the following exercises five to ten times each, keeping your forehead and body relaxed at all times. Close your eyes after each set of exercises and rest them for a moment.

1. Gently move your eyes up as far as they will go, then down as far as they will go.
2. Move your eyes as far to the right as they will, go, then as far to the left as they will go.
3. Move them diagonally up to your right as far as they will comfortably go, then diagonally down to your left.
4. Move them diagonally up to your left as far as they will go, then diagonally down to your right as far as is comfortable.
5. Now imagine the face of a clock in front of you. Make semicircles with your eyes from the 9 o'clock position through 12 o'clock and on to 3 o'clock; go back in reverse order. Make semicircles from the 9 o'clock position down through 6 o'clock, on to 3 o'clock, and reverse, returning to the starting position.
6. Finally, move your eyes several times around in a clockwise direction (passing through all the points on the clock). Reverse your direction and go counterclockwise several times. Proceed easily and with no strain.

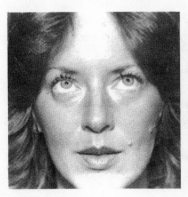  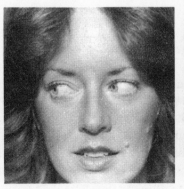 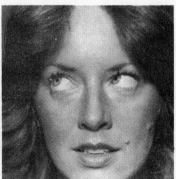

7. After finishing, cup your eyes with your hands (do not press them against your eyes) and allow your eyes to rest completely in darkness. Do this for at least one full minute. You can rest during the Eye Exercises whenever any strain is felt at all and not only at the conclusion of the exercises.

The Eye Exercises will greatly strengthen the eyes by increasing circulation of the vital-force to the eyes and toning the optic nerves. If, at any time, strain is felt during the exercises, gently massage your eyes with your fingertips and rest them in complete darkness.

THE LION POSE (*SIMHASANA*)

Sit comfortably on the floor in Kneeling Posture. In one complete motion, exhale (contracting your abdominal muscles in as far as possible), sticking your tongue out as far as possible (*feeling* the pull from inside your throat all the way to the end of your tongue); open your eyes and let them bulge outward; tense your whole body; and stiffen your arms, stretching your fingers widely apart. Hold for a few seconds and then repeat several times.

The Lion Pose is most useful for cleansing the throat area, and it can help cure a sore throat naturally by encouraging the blood to flow in increased volume to this area and to carry away toxins accumulated there. This posture should be done ten to fifteen times if the slightest bit of discomfort is ever felt in the throat area. It will encourage vital-force to flow upward more strongly and circulation to improve in the area of the head, thus discouraging any indisposition felt there.

SCALP EXERCISE

Sit comfortably on the floor and allow your body to become still and your mind to quiet down. Gently grasp your hair at its roots on the top of your head and pull until a slight resistance is felt. Pull your scalp gently back and forth several times. Proceed slowly over your entire head in the same manner until every part of your scalp has been massaged. The looser your scalp is, the more relaxed and easy-going you probably are at the moment.

The Scalp Exercise will increase the flow of vital-force to the head. Circulation will improve, the hair will become more healthy, and the massaging will have a restful and quieting effect upon the mind.

PRANAYAMA

Prana (vital-force) is the essential element from which all things in the universe are formed. *Prana* not only forms the body but also flows through it to animate and enliven it. When *prana* flows unevenly in the system and in strong force, one can usually be found involved in restless activity, with thoughts constantly racing through the mind. When prana flows weakly, one is usually lethargic and inclined towards laziness. If one can learn to control the flow of *prana* and life force in his system, he can also learn to control his thoughts and the eventual direction his life will take, once he has assumed responsibility for his actions.

To practice *pranayama* means to practice this control and regulation of the flow of vital-force in the body, and the easiest way to accomplish this is by controlling the breath and breathing (which will thereby affect the flow of life force in the system on all levels). When the breath is controlled, the flow of *prana* in the body is regulated and controlled. The body is then able to calm down and be still, and the mental activity can begin to subside. When *prana* moves in great force, the thought process begins anew. When *prana* slows down, the mind becomes more still and the thoughts become more subtle, the currents in the body become more balanced, and the body is able to remain motionless much more easily than is usually the case. Eventually all currents in the body will become harmonized through the continued practice of *pranayama*. This will encourage all of the vital-force to flow upward in the body in great volume, giving one a bright and vital appearance and almost unlimited every potential.

It is useful to conclude your practice of the *Yogasanas* with one or two *pranayama* exercises. Included in this section are two of the more simple *pranayamas* which most of you will find easy to do and beneficial to your system. Complete Breathing, the Cleansing Breath, and the Retaining Breath (all listed in the warmup section at the beginning of the book) are also *pranayamas* which could be repeated at this time if you so wish. There are, of course, more difficult *pranayamas* than those listed here, but you would be best advised to avoid such strenuous breathing exercises unless under the *personal* guidance of a *qualified* teacher. Such activity is unwise, because it often awakens in a student strong energy flows which are too powerful for him to handle without correct knowledge and competent personal guidance. As in all things, the moderate path in practice of *pranayama* is the wisest one for most people.

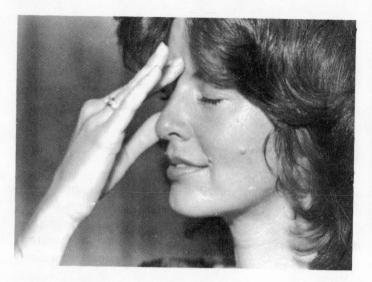 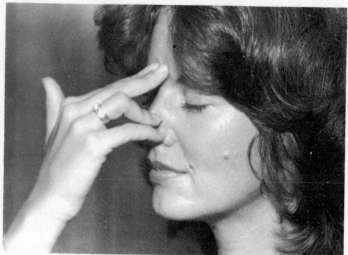

ALTERNATE NOSTRIL BREATHING (*ANULOMA VILOMA PRANAYAMA*)

Relax in a comfortable Sitting Posture with your spine erect, eyes closed, and attention focused within. Inhale and exhale completely two or three times to deepen relaxation. Place the forefinger and middle finger of your right hand at the point between your eyebrows. Exhale gently and completely, using your thumb to close your right nostril.

Pause for a moment before slowly and evenly inhaling through your left nostril; close that nostril with your third and fourth fingers, retain your breath for a moment; and exhale completely through your right nostril. Breathe deeply into your thoracic cavity throughout the entire process.

Pause for as long as is comfortable, inhale gently through your right nostril; hold a few moments, and exhale through your left nostril. Continue in this way for nine or ten rounds, keeping your attention on your breathing and remaining totally centered within. (Be especially aware during moments of non-breathing. At such times you can often receive insight into subtle areas of life if you are relaxed and open.) In time, the number of rounds you practice can be increased, but never to the point of exertion or becoming spaced-out. To go beyond the point of comfort would be to ignore the guidelines of gentleness, moderation, and respect for your body. Allow your body's tolerance for the exercises to increase naturally. In this way you will stay relaxed, in tune with yourself totally, and will cause no unnecessary strain on your body or nervous system.

Alternate Nostril Breathing is a powerful yet simple exercise that anyone can practice. Normally, in the course of a day, the breath flows more strongly through one nostril for a time, then switches to the opposite nostril on a regular schedule. But quite often the breath may not be flowing freely in both sides of the nostrils, and the passages may be obstructed with mucus due to improper diet or lack of body cleansing. Naturally this upsets the flow of *prana* in the body, contributing to an imbalance in the flow of currents and loss of harmony in the internal systems. (Hence the feeling of, "I don't know what's wrong, but I just don't have it together today.") Practicing Alternate Nostril Breathing will help cleanse the nasal passages and mucous membranes, as well as the nerve passageways (called *nadis*) which conduct life force in the body. Alternate Nostril Breathing will also help balance the flow of vital-force in the system, contributing to better balance in all internal systems, to calmness, and to steadiness. It will keep one centered, balanced, and in present-time awareness. This *pranayama* can be used anytime one feels jittery or off-center to help focus his attention and bring him back into the nowness of the moment.

Interesting to note is the flow of breath through the nostrils. Check with your hand held close to your nostrils to see in which side of your nose the current is flowing more strongly. When the breath flows more strongly through the right side, you are usually more goal-oriented, into action and activity, make decisions easily and quickly, and are generally more out-flowing or outer-directed. This is said to be the postive male current or the sun current. When your breath flows more strongly through your left nostril, you are usually more receptive, intuitive, quiet, inner directed, and influenced by your emotions. This is the moon current or the female negative current. (*Yogis* suggest that when you have an important decision to make in everyday affairs or business, you first check to see in which side of your nose the current is predominating. If it is in the left side, decisions could be rash or based on emotions and are best left to a later time. If the current is predominating in the right side of your nose, then any decisions you make will probably be practical ones and your intended projects will likely be seen to a quick, easy, and successful completion.)

"Learn to tell the difference between
God's will and whim-guided will."
— Paramahansa Yogananda

THE BELLOWS BREATH (*BHASTRIKA*)

Bhastrika means "the bellows," and this *pranayama* is so named because it sounds like the roaring bellows of the blacksmith when correctly executed. It is a powerful *pranayama* and should not be performed when you are overly tired or your physical system is not up to par.

Begin with your spine erect in a comfortable sitting posture (sitting is especially important if you are a smoker, as you may be inclined to become a little dizzy with the rigorous complete breathing). Exhale completely and vigorously, allowing air to come back into your lungs naturally. Put your attention at the tip of your nose and continue to exhale vigorously, each time forcing the air out of your lungs with a rapid bellows action. (If you place your hand a few inches under your nose, you will be able to tell if you are breathing correctly.) Concentrate more on your exhalations than your inhalations; the air will refill the lungs naturally with each breath. To begin, inhale and exhale in this manner for ten cycles. But proceed *slowly* and give your body time to increase its endurance and capacity to handle more cycles. This is most important. Never strain or push yourself to the point of giddiness. Always stop short of these points. Finally, inhale completely, exhale completely, close your eyes, and rest in the silence, observing changes within due to this *pranayama* and being totally aware of the moment.

Bhastrika will force stale air out of the lungs and encourage a more complete flow of vital-force throughout the system. It will also recharge the system with energy.

Both of the *pranayamas* on these pages are powerful exercises which directly affect the flow of life force within your body. Never use them as games to see how far you can push your body. To do so would be foolish and dangerous and would neglect the basic yogic rules of patience and gentleness. Always approach any *pranayama* exercises with respect and caution. Properly and consciously practiced, they are entirely safe and most beneficial.

CONCLUDING PRACTICE – RELAXATION AND MEDITATION

It is a good idea to make a point of concluding each and every practice session with a sufficiently long relaxation exercise in which you consciously relax each and every part of your body, or you can conclude your practice with meditation, which will have an even deeper effect. In this way, spending a few minutes being totally still and silent, allowing your body to relax completely, your mind to float, and your mental activity to subside as much as possible, the transition back to everyday living will be a smooth one. It will give you time to absorb all the benefits of the postures you have just practiced before you once again direct your attention to everyday living.

During the practice of *Yogasanas*, you have been totally absorbed in your own self, in the totality of your being and your own immediate space: your inner world. To get up, walk off, and suddenly resume daily activities would be a tremendous shock to the nervous system and would leave you dazed, off-center, and out of the flow of things. Spending a few minutes at the end of practice in total silence can be an invaluable aid in helping you shift gears smoothly from inner concentration to outer activity. It will allow you to carry the awareness you have developed during practice into your daily life and activities, enhancing the quality of your life and everything that you do. It is then that you are able to become one of the truly conscious persons who flows with life, spending your time wisely and functioning freely and with understanding, making a valuable contribution to your world and the people whose lives you touch.

To get straight and clear with one's own self initially is the secret to living life consciously and with purpose.

147

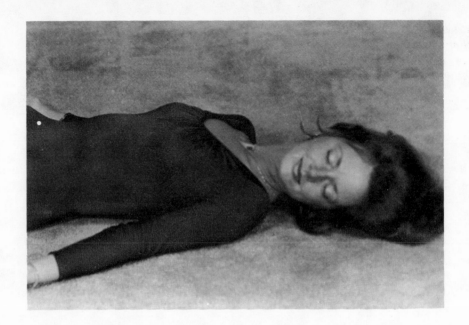

RELAXING THE BODY TOTALLY

Here is a technique you can use to encourage the complete relaxation of your mind and body. Lie in the Corpse Pose with your *entire* spine stretched out on the floor (pay attention to your lower back and neck areas, making sure there is no stress in your lower back and that your neck is flat on the floor. Bend your knees if you encounter any noticeable distress in your lower back). Have no part of your body touching another. Spread your legs and arms out from your body, with your palms up for receptivity and openness to life. Roll your neck back and forth until it comes to a stop and the placement of your head and neck feels comfortable and natural.

Close your eyes and turn your attention within. Take several deep, complete breaths to further relax your body. Notice that the energy in your body will follow the flow of your attention. Direct your attention first to your toes. Wiggle them, locate them in your body, and really *feel* where they are from inside yourself. Say, *I am relaxing my toes*. Withdraw your attention from your toes and let them relax completely. Be the observer and watch your toes relax, knowing that each successive part of your body will listen and respond to this command as you continue. Once your toes are relaxed, there is no need to think of them again or to move them at all.

Turn your attention now to your feet and ankles. Realize their location in your body by flexing and relaxing them several times. Really *feel* the reality of them. Say, *I am relaxing my feet and ankles*, and let them do so.

Bring your attention now to your calf muscles and the shin areas of your legs. Contract and relax these areas several times until you feel total identification with them. Relax them completely, withdrawing your attention and vital-force from these areas entirely. Proceed easily and be gentle with your body. Flow smoothly and be unhurried, as if in slow motion, with an absence of thoughts other than directing your body to relax.

Move now to your knees and thigh areas. Contract and relax your knees and thighs several times, then allow them to sink into the floor. Withdraw your attention from these areas. Your legs should remain completely motionless, not moving again throughout the entire exercise.

Your feet and legs may become numb and without feeling at this point. Notice how heavy they seem, almost as though they have become glued to the floor.

Pull your attention up to your buttocks and genital area. Contract and relax these areas several times, all the while taking care to *feel* where these body parts are and to identify fully with them as parts of your body. After contracting them a few times, relax the buttocks and the genitals totally. Allow this part of your body to sink heavily into the floor, withdrawing your attention and vital-force completely from it.

Concentrate now on the abdominal area. Inhale, filling your stomach with air and causing it to expand. Pause for a moment. Exhale completely through your mouth, allowing the stomach to flatten and muscles in this area to become still and at rest. Forget this area entirely.

Give full attention now to your chest area. Become aware of your heartbeat and lungs. Inhale deeply, expanding your lungs and chest; exhale through your mouth and allow your chest to sink down into the floor, your lungs to relax, and your heartbeat to slow down. Feel your chest relax.

Turn your attention to your fingers. Locate them by flexing and relaxing them several times, finally allowing them to stop and remain still, with no need to move again.

Tune into your hands and wrists. Move them a little to locate them in your body; relax them completely. Withdraw your attention and vital-force from these areas totally. Let your hands be still and do not move them again.

Identify now fully with your forearms. Tighten and relax the muscles here several times, finally saying, *I am relaxing my forearms*. Observe as your forearms respond to this suggestion. Withdraw your attention from these areas and forget them entirely.

Bring your attention up now to your elbows and upper arms. Tighten and relax the muscles here several times, finally withdrawing your attention from these areas and allowing your elbows and upper arms to sink heavily into the floor.

Think next of your entire spinal column. Locate it in your body. *Feel* the reality of it. Let your entire spine relax, one vertebra at a time, starting with your tailbone, continuing to your lower back, moving up to the middle back, and finally to your upper back. Watch the vital-force move up your spinal column and notice the loss of sensation that follows as you withdraw your attention from each vertebra up the spinal column. Feel your spine sink into the floor and your body become heavier and heavier with each moment. Remove your attention from this area entirely, once your entire spine has relaxed.

Tune in now with your neck and shoulder area. Locate and feel them in your body. Gently press your shoulder blades together several times, then relax them totally. Feel the tension leave this area of your body as your body relaxes and attention is withdrawn from it.

Think now of the throat area. With conscious intent, locate your throat by moving it slightly and feel the reality of its existence in your body. After you have tuned into this area, allow your throat to relax and forget it entirely.

Jut your chin out as far as possible and move it around. Relax it completely. Press your lips together tightly and pucker them a few times, then let them relax. Locate your tongue and move it a little. Let it relax. Let your jawbone relax; do not allow your teeth to grind together at all. Allow your jaw to sag if it wants. Now forget all these relaxed areas completely.

Wrinkle your nose slowly several times and then relax it completely. Suck in your cheeks; allow them to relax. Withdraw your attention from your nose and cheeks and do not think of them or move them again.

Become aware of your eyes. Open and shut them several times, until they close easily without fluttering. Withdraw your attention from them and forget them entirely.

Wrinkle your forehead several times and allow it to relax completely. This muscle of the body, if held tense, tends to encourage the rest of the body to tense automatically. Make sure your forehead is entirely relaxed, then pull your attention up and away from this area.

Allow your scalp muscles to relax totally. Actually feel them doing so. Feel a coolness envelop the entire body now as your attention is withdrawn from body consciousness. Allow your vital-force to come up to the top of your body and envision it coming out of the top of your head, as though it were being sucked up into a tube.

At this point in your relaxation, it is useful to mentally direct your attention once more to each part of your body, starting with your toes all the way up to your head, to be certain that all tension has been completely removed from your body and that none remains unnoticed. You must be totally aware of all the parts of your body in order to be able to locate any tension contained in it. You must be able to *feel* the reality of each part; such awareness will give you the ability to spot any blockages in the flow of your vital-force to any of your body parts. At those times you can turn off the tension in that part (or parts) of your body as simply as turning off a light switch, by directing your attention to the afflicted area and telling it to relax. Take a few moments now to recheck your body thoroughly. Do not move any part of your body in which you may locate any remaining tension, however, but, instead, send your attention to the tight area and mentally direct it to relax. Observe as it responds. Your body will always respond to your suggestions, and it is easy to see, as you relax each part of your body, that you are in control of the thoughts in your mind, and, in turn, your own body responses. After rechecking your body thoroughly, forget it entirely and rest easily.

During this conscious relaxation, the body may at first seem heavy, as though it were a part of the floor. As more time is spent in relaxation, the sensation may turn to one of lightness. One may become aware of disengaging from his body, floating around and observing his surroundings. It is interesting at such times to imagine how it might be if one came into the room and observed his body lying on the floor as an outsider would, without any emotion or attachment to it. When viewed simply as a part of the manifesting world, the body ceases to be such an obsession to the person who is wearing it. He realizes that if he is the one who is observing the body at this moment, he cannot possibly be his body only. He must be greater than mere physical matter and more than his changing emotions. In total relaxation, with surrender and full awareness of the moment, revealing insights and realizations can occur about the truth of life, giving one peace and contentment with all that is, as well as new enthusiasm and purpose for living.

To deepen relaxation even further, you might imagine being on an elevator on the tenth floor of a building. Feel your body become more relaxed as the elevator moves from the tenth floor, to the ninth, eighth, seventh, sixth, fifth, fourth, third, second, and first. As the elevator comes to a stop, know that all the tension is drained from your body and that relaxation is complete. Perhaps you would prefer to imagine being at one of your favorite spots with the sun shining brightly. If so, feel the warmth of the sun relaxing your body and stilling your mind as it radiates on each part of your body. Or imagine being on a sailboat in a calm and gentle sea. Feel your body relax progressively as the boat floats gently over the friendly rolling waves. Perhaps you might visualize a sable paintbrush painting soft circles around your body, relaxing your body and removing tension from each part that it encircles. You can use any favorite technique that you find useful in relaxing your body. Let your imagination soar and discover what is most appealing and effective for you. After relaxing your body consciously, remain still in *Savasana*.

This kind of *conscious sleep* can actually be more beneficial to the mind and body than the actual hours spent in sleep each night. This occurs because, with conscious relaxation, stress and tension are deliberately removed

from body and mind first, which then affords complete rest and total relaxation to the entire system. Five minutes properly spent in conscious relaxation can be the equivalent of five or six usual sleep hours. The body is free of stress and the mental processes of the mind are stilled. This is a most revitalizing and desirable state in which to be resting but yet observing everything that occurs from within one's self in a detached viewpoint: seeing everything as it truly is.

After at least five minutes, begin to come back slowly to body awareness. Allow your attention to center in your upper scalp initially. *Feel* the vital-force as it begins to make its descent back down into your body through your head, down into your arms, through your chest and spinal column, into your abdomen, through your pelvis and on into your legs, all the way down your legs, and into the extremities of your toes. Watch and feel it as it animates and enlivens your entire body. Let it come in slowly and reach every extremity in your body. Since tension and mental stress have been eradicated and the currents in your body can now flow naturally and evenly, *prana* is able to flow evenly to all parts of your body, giving you more energy and vitality and a brighter physical appearance. Feel the awakened energy in your body. Assured now that vital-force flows with no restrictions and that all systems in your body function perfectly and in harmony, you will realize that all *is* well. Silently bless the world at this time and anyone who comes to mind. Feel in harmony with your world.

Then gently wake your body up, taking a vital lesson from the animal and cat world: stretching each part of your body, yawning fully, and gently bringing yourself back to full body awareness, but with a new sense of peace and serenity.

This technique for relaxation can be used anytime during the day when you feel physically or emotionally drained. All you need is a quiet spot to lie down and four or five minutes to consciously relax each part of your body. These few minutes can refresh you and improve your mental attitude. If your time is very limited, you can relax major portions of your body at one time (the entire right leg and foot, for instance).

*"Constantly inquire into the
reality of your own being."
— Ramana Maharishi*

THE QUICK CORPSE POSE

The Quick Corpse Pose can also be used when time for relaxation is short and is a good way to begin longer relaxation sessions. Lie supine, totally relaxed once more, and take several complete breaths. Consciously tense *every* muscle in your body, retain your breath, and raise your legs, arms, head, shoulders, and back up off the floor until your entire body is resting on your buttocks. Hold for a moment, all the while really *feeling* and identifying with the tenseness in all parts of your body. Exhale completely, letting your body drop back to the floor, and relax. Do this two or three times, then remain motionless for at least a minute, observing your body as it relaxes and keeping your attention on your breathing, so as not to incur unwanted mental distractions.

There may be times when you find yourself so exhausted or strung-out that you cannot talk yourself through any relaxation technique; at such times you are literally wiped-out. If this occurs, you may find it helpful to have a friend talk you through the routine. Better still is to tape a session with your own voice to use whenever necessary. It matters little which method is used. Most important is to take the time to relax and unwind whenever necessary.

154

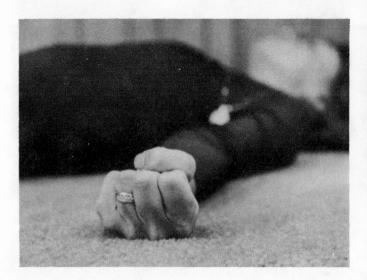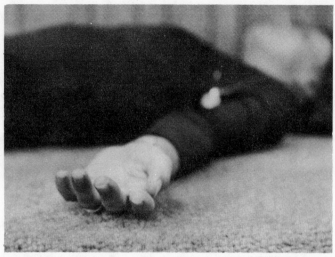

HOUSEKEEPING

If, sometimes before practicing complete relaxation, you find your mind preoccupied with a personal problem you cannot seem to shake, you can practice a little *housekeeping* to release the problem. Lie in the Corpse Pose and extend your left arm out from your body with the palm turned upwards. Think of your problem, picture it in your mind's eye, and reduce it down in size so that it will fit right in the palm of your outstretched hand. Open your left hand and flatten your fingers firmly on the floor. Take your problem (or problems) and mentally place them in the palm of your hand. Really *feel* and see the emotion of it. Inhale and exhale completely a few times. Slowly make a fist with your outstreched hand and imagine that you are shattering your problem in it, breaking the problem into a million pieces. Slowly begin to open your fingers, and, with each exhalation, imagine that your breath is blowing the pieces of this problem away until it no longer exists. Continue to relax your body, bit by bit, as you did in the Corpse Posture. Getting rid of the emotions of a problem will help your body relax. Then your mind can become still and the flow of *prana* in your system can slow down, making total relaxation much easier. When your mind is agitated with thoughts, you will find it difficult to remain still, since the uneven flow of *prana* will tend to make you restless and keep you in motion. Be certain that you observe and realize the connection between the flow of life force in your system and your state of mind and degree of calmness.

RECHARGING EXERCISES

Sometimes one needs to be able to relax his mind and body in a very short period of time. The next four exercises are designed to do that and to recharge the body quickly with vital-force through relaxation and creative visualization. There is an exercise for each of the elements: earth, water, fire, and air. Often one will discover that he has a natural preference for one (or more) of these. Sometimes this has to do with which element predominates in the natal birth chart or with which element is weak or missing and whose presence would have a balancing or stabilizing effect upon the system. These exercises can be used alone to recharge one's psychic batteries rapidly, or they can be used at the end of a longer relaxation session to bring one back into total body awareness and allow him to emerge with full use of his energy reserves. It is always useful for each person to decide just which exercise feels best for him and to use his own imagination to create exercises for each of the elements that have special appeal for him.

FOR THE EARTH ELEMENT

Lie in the Corpse Pose with your spine stretched out entirely and your eyes closed. Watch your breath coming in and going out your nostrils. Take several complete breaths, allowing your mind to become quiet and your body to become still and relaxed. Bring to mind and reflect upon a favorite spot you like to visit: be it the beach and ocean, a lake, a mountain site, a waterfall, a canyon, a quiet garden, a grove of peaceful trees, or whatever works and makes you feel calm, happy, and serene. In your mind's eye, envision yourself at this special place. Take note of all the surroundings and let the image become very real in your imagination. Feel the warmth or the coolness, the beauty, the vitality, the healthfulness, and the peacefulness of this location. Let your body become one with all of the surroundings. With each inhalation, know that your body is absorbing the healing vibrations of this special place, all of its beauty and its vitality. With each exhalation, know that your body is becoming more and more relaxed. Continue to breathe in health, vitality, and serenity and to relax your body more and more each time you exhale. Do this for at least one full minute. Then, feel the oneness with this place again; bring your attention back gently to the cycle of your breathing and to body awareness; stretch every muscle in your body gently and fully; open your eyes; and slowly sit up again, knowing that vital-force now flows unimpeded in your system and that you are healthy, relaxed, and radiantly alive.

FOR THE WATER ELEMENT

Lie completely relaxed in the Corpse Pose with your attention on your breathing. Take several complete breaths, breathing deeply into your thoracic cavity and allowing your body and mind to settle down. Continue to breathe fully in this manner and picture, in your mind's eye, a peaceful pool of water surrounded by beautiful trees. Imagine yourself standing on a small ledge a few feet above the pool, holding a large heavy ball. In slow motion, imagine that you are easily lifting the ball high up over your head and slowly lowering it until, just in front of your body, you release it and let it fall into the water. See the splash and the spray of water flying into the air as the ball breaks the surface. Continue to watch, in slow motion action, as the ball falls to the bottom of the pond and the water closes in on it again. Watch the circles of ripplets begin to glide across the smooth surface. Let yourself become mesmerized by the quiet, continuous rings of ripplets circling outwards. Continue to watch until all the ripplets have disappeared and the surface is smooth again. Feel the coolness, calmness, and the serenity of the water. Lie still, allowing every pore of your body to become further relaxed and tranquilized by the image of this now-calm water. Then, gently bring your attention back to your breathing and slowly allow your attention to come out and reestablish contact with your environment. Open your eyes and return to your daily activities. Know that you are fully relaxed and recharged with vital-force and flowing appropriately with life, moment to moment.

FOR THE FIRE ELEMENT

Lie in the Corpse Pose with your body stretched out and fully relaxed, your eyes closed, and your awareness on your cycle of breathing in and out through your nostrils. Breathe in and out fully several times to further encourage relaxation. Continue breathing fully in this manner and picture yourself, again in your mind's eye, in front of a blazing fire in a huge, over-sized fireplace. Watch the flames as they leap higher and higher. Feel the warmth as the fire continues to burn brightly. See all the colors, bright and subdued, contained in the flames themselves. Continue to watch and to breathe deeply and evenly. Then, with each inhalation, feel that you are drawing in the light, energy, brightness, and vitality of this fire. With each exhalation, feel that your body is becoming more and more relaxed. Continue to do this for at least one minute. Tension will be drained from your body, so that vital-force will begin to circulate completely in deeper layers in your entire system to enliven your body and give it brightness and vitality. It will be easy to release all of the secondary tension in the system at such times (tension which is not needed to accomplish a task at hand). Your system will be cleansed and cleared of any blockages in vital-force and available energy, and you will have full use of primary tension (tension that is necessary in the body to accomplish the jobs at hand). Slowly bring your attention back to your breathing cycle and come back to full body awareness and your immediate surroundings. Know that all systems function perfectly. Open your eyes and go back into the stream of Life, revitalized and enthusiastically participating with It.

FOR THE AIR ELEMENT

Close your eyes and relax your body completely in *Savasana*. Keep your attention centered on your breathing; breathe completely and fully to encourage further body relaxation and stillness in your mind. Visualize yourself, in your mind's eye, floating lightly in the air, buoyed up by light, fluffy clouds. Continue to breathe evenly. Imagine a thin aura of light completely surrounding your entire body. Watch it and become aware of all the colors contained within it. Imagine that this aura progressively becomes brighter and brighter, extending further away from your body but still surrounding it. Feel it pulsate and feel its magnetic energy as it fills the space around you. Think of your body as being a sponge, with every pore and cell open to receive the life-giving energy from the surrounding air. Continue the slow, rhythmic breathing, and, with each inhalation, think of receiving in through every cell of your system the lightness and brightness of the surrounding aura. Feel it penetrate and enliven your system. With each exhalation, know and feel that your body is becoming more and more relaxed and, with it, your mind becoming more still. Continue for a short time in this manner. Then, begin to bring your attention slowly back out again, centering first on your breathing, finally coming back to full body awareness. Know that your entire system is fully relaxed, recharged, and lightened by the loss of unnecessary tension in your body and mind. Open your eyes, sit up slowly, stretching all your muscles gently, and go about your daily business, flowing and responding easily from one moment to the next.

*"Everything in Nature contains
all the powers of Nature. Everything
is made of one hidden stuff."*
                    — Ralph Waldo Emerson

MEDITATION

Many, after practicing the different techniques for relaxation, will want to go further to the practice of meditation. The *Yogasanas, pranayamas*, and relaxation techniques will relax one's body and help him feel healthy, confident, and more in control of his life. Meditation will also relax the body and all its systems totally, as will the relaxation methods, but it will work in addition on the more subtle areas of one's being to awaken energy at much deeper levels. It is to the practice of meditation that *Hatha Yoga* naturally leads, since one of the main purposes of this practice to to prepare the body and calm the mind so that one is able to remain motionless while in meditation. *Hatha Yoga* often awakens dormant energy deep within one's being and inclines him towards further self-discovery, and, at this point in practice, one may discover an insistent urge to delve just a bit deeper in his study.

The practice of *Yogasanas* gives one new awareness and insights into his life, he learns that he can control his mind and his thoughts, and he sees that his real nature is more than just his body and mind. So it is logical for one to begin to seek answers to deeper and more serious questions that will contribute to a life of further meaning and greater understanding. Meditation is the place to find these answers. Exactly what is meditation?

Meditation is simply the turning of one's attention to the inmost center of his being and there resting for a time, emerging refreshed and clear on all levels, and then easily flowing back again into the stream of life. The practice of *Yogasanas* strengthens the body and purifies the nerves, making it possible for one to remain still for long periods of time and to direct all of his life force within, instead of continuously flowing out in daily activities and restless movement. The practice of *pranayamas* enables one to learn to control the vital-force in his body and to encourage this vital-force to flow upwards evenly, calming the body and stilling the mind. Both *Yogasanas* and *pranayamas* may incline him towards an inner quest or search, though he might never have realized such an inclination before. Questions may begin to arise in his mind, such as, "What is the purpose of life?" "Why am I here?" "Who am I really?" "What is my real nature?" The answers to these questions and many more may be found in the stillness and the quietness that is meditation.

One often finds himself identified heavily with his body and emotional nature, thinking incorrectly that his body and emotions are what he is. Because of such incorrect thinking, it is useful to disconnect daily from the senses and feeling nature and become centered once again in the real nature of one's being. Meditation is the time to do this, to become fully grounded in the awareness of one's true nature, and then to emerge and participate consciously in life, contributing more because of increased awareness and openness with Life. One sees clearly, through his practice of *Yoga*, that he is more than his body; it is his vehicle for expression in this world. He is more than his mind; think how often one says, "I think I'll change my mind." This alone should tell him that he is not the mind because he has the power to change it! One practices, during daily time allotted to the *asanas*, being the *witness* of all the thoughts and feelings that arise in the mind. But these impressions come and go; they are not permanent; so they cannot be the real person. Anything that is subject to change cannot be the real person.

Then, exactly what is one's real nature? He is an individualization of all there is. He has taken on a body and personality in order to express in this world, but the body and personality are not his real and changeless nature. The real being is the soul nature: bright, shining, clear, and living forever, even as God does. The soul nature is the clear, permanent part of one that knows, simply *by knowing*, by intuition, when he is sure of the answer to a question. It is the clear part of one's nature that observes vividly and rationally, without emotional entanglement or personal will. It is to this bright, clear, shining center that meditation takes one and affords him rest.

One will have problems only when he forgets to live out of this still small center, perhaps because of overinvolvement with the senses, physical illness or disabilities that tie him too concretely into his body and personality, or procrastination and laziness that cause him to be negligent in his practice of meditation.

Meditation is simple enough for anyone to practice, once he is so inclined. It involves setting aside twenty to thirty minutes in the morning and evening to rest consciously at one's inmost center. There is nothing mysterious about the process; it simply must be done to be experienced. One should not sit for very long periods to begin with, because more may be dragged up from the unconscious than he might be able to handle at that time (this would manifest perhaps as jittery nerves or extreme restlessness, nothing dangerous or frightening, but still an unnecessary experience). One should not overdo or push too quickly with meditation, just as he did not in *Hatha practice*. Once again, moderation and gentleness are always the guidelines. One should proceed faithfully but steadily each day, and, as the nervous system is cleansed and the mind becomes clearer, he will realize more fulfilled living, a truer sense of all rightness with his own self, an increase in his creativity, more enthusiasm and interest in his daily life, and revealing insights into the real nature of life and all that is.

BEGINNING

When you first begin to meditate, you can sit on the floor in one of the Sitting Postures (a cushion placed under your buttocks will help ease any stress you might notice in the area of your hips or legs). If you are uncomfortable on the floor, you can sit in a straight chair with firm support (sitting on the edge, crossing your feet at the ankles, hands on your knees). You might begin by practicing a little Alternate Nostril Breathing to help balance the currents in your system and calm you down. Make sure your entire spine is straight and tall, close your eyes gently, and bring your thumb and forefinger together, resting your hands on your knees. Locking your thumb and forefinger in the simple *Chin Mudra* will encourage your energies to circulate completely within your own system. It will lock your vital-force in your system and enable you more easily to remain self-contained and inward flowing. Flow your attention within now, focusing it upon one point. An easy way to do this is by watching your breath coming in through the tip of your nostrils and watching it flow back out again, as you did in the *asanas*. Be expectant and open but have no anxiety for results. Just watch your body as it breathes in and out, being particularly attentive to those times when your breathing may stop, as it naturally will, for short times (perhaps only a second or two at first), when all your systems are perfectly balanced and in harmony. At such times as these, simply observe as your body and mind are totally stilled and *prana* slows down; these are the times when breakthroughs in consciousness and awareness may be experienced. If and when any thoughts and feelings arise in your mind, pay them no heed. Observe them without judgment and let them go. Trying to stop them will only encourage more thoughts to arise. Instead, return to watching your breathing, keeping yourself centered and conscious in this way.

It is normal for thoughts and feelings to arise as long as any restlessness remains in one's nature, especially when he is just a beginner at meditation. One should stay with his practice and always look beyond any of these mental or emotional impressions. He should remember they are only impressions and have no reality of their own. In time, they will be neutralized if practice is continued, and one will experience the clear state of being. Here is where he will find answers to the purpose of life and anything else he wishes to know. He need only meditate twenty to thirty minutes a day without fail. One great teacher has stated that if one will truthfully observe this practice for six months, he will be hooked by it, unable to give it up. There will be such an improvement in his quality of living and his inner life that it will not be possible for him to let his practice go. Try it for yourself and see what happens.

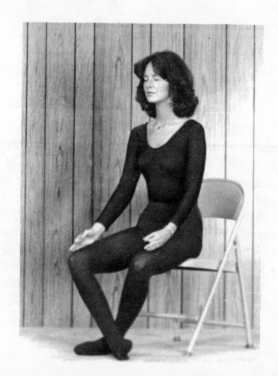

"There is a quiet place
within each person. It
is from this place we
view our world in
perfect peace and poise."
— Roy Eugene Davis

FOCUSING ATTENTION

A useful preliminary technique to help clear your mind and focus your attention is *Tratakam*, also called steady gazing. This can be done while seated comfortably in a dark room with a lighted candle in front of you. Simply gaze at the candle as long as you are able to without blinking. When the urge to blink becomes very strong, rub your palms together, close your eyes, and rest (do not press) your palms gently over your eyes. The afterimage of the candle will be seen at the Third Eye Center. Gaze at the candle several times again, then rest. You can do this for as long as it is comfortable. *Tratakam* can also be practiced in a lighted room by staring at any single chosen object until your eyes begin to burn, or you may focus on any object outside in nature. This simple exercise will teach you to focus your attention and may introduce you to the inner lights that some people (but not all of them) perceive at the Third Eye during meditation. (If you should perceive these lights, simply observe them without getting caught up in them. They are like mental impressions in that they have no reality of their own. Keeping your attention centered will help you get past any phenomena you perceive, no matter how pleasing it may be or how much fun you may be having—or vice versa.) Remember, the purpose of meditation is to become clear and not to get caught up in side trips along the way.

There are other techniques for keeping your attention centered and in present-time awareness. One useful method is *mantra* meditation. You can practice this technique by sitting in a very quiet place and listening deeply within. Before long you will hear sounds in the inner ear. Initial sounds may be of the electrical activity of the nervous system. After a while you may hear a steady and stronger sound. Whatever is heard can be taken as a point of focus for the attention. Do not strain while using this process, relax into the sound, and allow yourself to be consciously absorbed in it. This is the most direct route to inner peace and satisfaction.

Sometimes a specific mantra is given by a teacher. All mantras derive their potency from the primal sound of *Aum* (OM). An easy mantra for the purpose of relaxation and concentration is *So-Ham*. Just sit in your meditation position. Be relaxed and flow attention gently to the Third Eye Center. Observe the natural breathing cycle. When you breathe in, mentally listen to *So* and when you breathe out mentally listen to *Ham* (Hum). This is all you do while using this mantra. Surrender to the Third Eye Center, be relaxed and flow with the mantra. Do not mentally affirm the mantra, just "listen" to it in your mind as though it were surfacing there on its own.

At times, when one is very relaxed and inwardly absorbed, one will see a light at the Third Eye Center. The inner lights are due to the movements of vital-force in the system and are not of themselves of any great value. But, if a light is steadily perceived at the Third Eye it can be used as a point upon which to focus attention and, in this way, assist the meditation process.

A meditation ideal is to experience such total conscious relaxation that the inner process continues spontaneously without personal effort. After resting in the peak experience for a duration, one's attention will naturally incline outward.

It is most useful to approach your meditation session as you do your *Yogasanas*: relaxed, open and expectant, with no preconceived expectations. Some people see brilliant lights and vivid visions; others see nothing, but they experience a perfect sense of peacefulness and being. What happens will vary with each person and is best left un-talked about except with one's personal teacher, if he has one. Meditation should be thought of as a very private and personal time between the meditator and his Maker, and too much talk about inner experiences can take away some of the meaning and significance they have for him. Meditation is a time of listening, emptying one's self of all his preconceived notions, attitudes, and opinions, and being open to allow Life itself to direct him again. What happens for each person is exactly right for the moment; as in *Hatha Yoga*, especially so in meditation. One is exactly where he should be, and all experiences necessary to help him along the path of self-discovery will be natural and forthcoming. It is useful for one to remember to acknowledge that whatever is necessary for his personal inner unfoldment will occur at exactly the precise moment in order to fulfill his particular destiny or life plan. All one need do is sit back, relax, and observe the process consciously as it unfolds around him. In this way, he will not be fighting Life or demanding of It; he will be flowing with It. If one's mind becomes engaged in thought during meditation and gets off the track, all he need do is gently bring his attention back to watching his breath, repeating his *mantra*, watching the inner light, or listening to the inner sound (OM). The process is simple and it cannot fail. The proof will come with continued practice. The quality of living and the peacefulness within one's self will improve to such a degree that he will not want or be able to forget his practice. The anticipation and quiet joy he experiences will be so all encompassing that he will look forward to his practice time each day with pleasure and expectancy, a time not to be missed, and every bit as real and satisfying as his outer world. In fact, it will progressively add Reality to his everyday world.

Remember, during the practice of meditation, that anything perceived, whether it be happy, sad, exhilarating, pleasurable, lights, visions, etc., is not real in itself and is therefore subject to change. It is only when one rises above the impressions of his mind that he will experience the clear state of Being. This is the clear state of living wherein he is able to view life as it really is, clearly and objectively. The *yogis* call this state *samadhi*, which means to bring everything into evenness. Here is where one will experience the true nature of his own being. Here is where all his answers in life are to be found. Resting here, at one's inmost center, he will know beyond all doubt that everything *is* in its right place, that he is here to participate consciously in the joyous plan of Life, and that all is well with the universe. At such a time, anxiety, self-doubt, tension, guilt, resentment, and all that once restricted him in his expression can be released, and he can live his life fully cognizant that every monent in his life will count as long as he plays his role with conscious understanding. Upon such realization and practical living does living life, making every moment count, depend.

Practice meditation until you become proficient at it. It will be time well-spent.

"In the sublime serenity of pure consciousness the soul becomes established in and realizes its identity with God."
— *Lahiri Mahasaya*

*I salute the supreme teacher, the Truth,
whose nature is bliss, who is the giver
of the highest happiness, who is pure
wisdom, who is beyond all qualities and
infinite like the sky, who is beyond words,
who is one and eternal, pure and still,
who is beyond all change and phenomena
and who is the silent witness to all our
thoughts and emotions—I salute Truth,
the supreme teacher.*

— Ancient Vedic Hymn

This page for your own notes:

*"Gladness of the heart is the life of man, and
the joyfulness of a man prolongeth his days."*
                    — The Apocrypha XXX, 22

This page for your own notes:

"The culture of love, the heavenly gift,
is the principal requisite for the attainment
of holy salvation; it is impossible for man
to advance a step toward the same without it."
— Swami Sri Yukteswar

This page for your own notes:

*"Believe that there is nothing greater than
Truth; nothing more precious, nothing sweeter
and nothing more lasting."*
— *Sri Satya Sai Baba*

This page for your own notes:

*"Under a golden brilliance the Face of Truth
    lies hidden.
Do Thou, O Protector, withdraw this cover
that I, devoted to Truth alone, may
realize it."*

— Isavasyopanisad